Insourcing

After the

Outsourcing

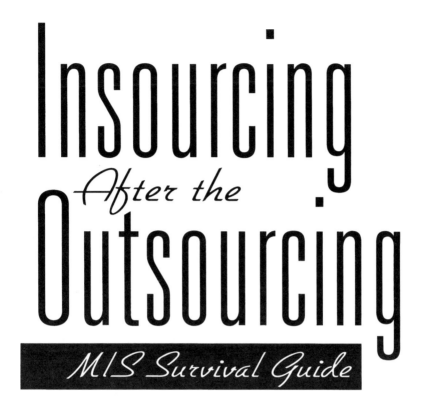

Insourcing
After the
Outsourcing

MIS Survival Guide

Robert B. Chapman and Kathleen Andrade

AMACOM
American Management Association
New York • Atlanta • Boston • Chicago • Kansas City • San Francisco • Washington, D.C.
Brussels • Mexico City • Tokyo • Toronto

658.05
C46i

This publication is designed to provide accurate and authoritative information in regard to the subject matter covered. It is sold with the understanding that the publisher is not engaged in rendering legal, accounting, or other professional service. If legal advice or other expert assistance is required, the services of a competent professional person should be sought.

Library of Congress Cataloging-in-Publication Data

Chapman, Robert B.
    Insourcing after the outsourcing : MIS survival guide / Robert B.
Chapman and Kathleen Andrade.
      p. cm.
    Includes index.
    ISBN 0-8144-0386-7
    1. Electronic data processing departments—Contracting out.
    2. Information resources management. I. Andrade, Kathleen.
    II. Title.
    HF5548.2.C472   1997
    658'.05—dc21   97–22507
                                                       CIP

Printing number

10 9 8 7 6 5 4 3 2 1

Contents

Preface

Outsourcing is a business process that affects many companies today. These companies are scrambling to accrue the benefits of removing MIS (Management Information System). Outsourcing gives an immediate benefit to the bottom line and provides companies with a known cost for the foreseeable future. It controls the costs of the MIS function, costs that have been burgeoning over the last several decades. It terminates the empire building taking place within many MIS departments. In short, outsourcing is management's dream of controlling MIS come true.

But what happens when outsourcing does not work for a company? What happens when costs continue to go up, or the level of service goes down, or both? What happens when outsourcing becomes the problem and not the solution?

It is always easy to go along with the crowd, and most times a company will continue to thrive using conventional wisdom as a guide. But in the case of the MIS function, it is crucial to the success of the company to consider the costs of going along for the ride. Before a company jumps into outsourcing, it needs to be sure it can jump back out.

> When You Run With the Crowd, Make Sure You Don't Slip.

In this book we consider the ramifications of outsourcing gone bad. This needs to be addressed now, before many more companies commit to outsourcing. The book reviews the general motivations behind outsourcing, discussing their appropriateness and general effects. It reviews what a company can expect from outsourcing during the early years of the contract. Then it addresses how outsourcing can start failing and when failure will probably start. Finally, it looks at insourcing the outsourced MIS functions, and it asks the questions a company needs to ask about returning the MIS function to the company environment. At the end, we discuss whether outsourcing was a good idea.

Each of these topics could span an entire book in itself. This book can be used as a guide to reviewing the most likely situations a company can find itself in. It can also be used to set a long-term direction for MIS. Each company should ask the obvious and appropriate questions regarding its own outsourcing situation.

Insourcing
After the
Outsourcing

1

Defining Outsourcing and Insourcing

MIS professionals are expected to be knowledgeable about outsourcing. As the months go by, many professionals are intimately entwined in the outsourcing trends. Even so, there are many who do not understand exactly what outsourcing is, possibly because the term has been used as an umbrella to encompass many different activities. *Insourcing,* on the other hand, is a new word, whose meaning is implied once *outsourcing* is defined.

The interesting thing about these words is not their meaning but the fact that the words themselves are new. When looked at from a historical perspective, it becomes apparent that outsourcing has its roots in facilities management, which was popular in the late 1960s and early 1970s. Unfortunately, facilities management became associated with the words *expensive* and *bad service.* Thus, it is not surprising that facilities management is no longer practiced in the mainstream MIS world.

While it would be wrong to say that *outsourcing* is just another word for *facilities management,* it is only wrong because the scope of outsourcing is so much more encompassing than facilities management ever was. It certainly looks to the casual observer as if outsourcing is simply a Madison Avenue twist on an old failure.

What Is Outsourcing?

Outsourcing is the movement of computer-related functions from within an organization to an external environment. The traditional outsourcing arrangement consists of taking computer operations out of a company and contracting them to a service bureau. But in fact, outsourcing encompasses much more than this. Outsourcing encompasses the movement of any part of MIS functionality to an outside agent. This is confusing because the operative words are *any* and *outside*, which imply much more than one typically assumes.

MIS consists of many different functions. The ones that come most quickly to mind are computer operations and systems development. Other functions are also part of MIS. These consist of product development for user departments, strategic planning for the corporation, maintenance programming, corporate communications (although this is often associated with facilities), and forecasting efforts of all different types. Outsourcing covers the movement of any or all of these functions from within an existing organization, either by department or company, to an outside agent.

Outsourcing Means MIS Has *Lost* Its Job.

An outside agent is typically a service bureau of some sort. But more and more today it is coming to mean a large consulting service such as EDS, IBM Global Services, and Andersen Consulting. However, an outside agent can also mean another organization within the same company. For instance, a marketing department can have its MIS function outsourced to the company's formal MIS department. Or an internal MIS department can be spun off as a separate company and take all the functions with it. So it can be seen that outsourcing means much more than one would historically expect.

Many Outsourcing Ventures Will Fail.

Outsourcing ventures can be classified according to their probability of success, as follows:

1. Candidates for (generally) successful outsourcing
   a. Data processing operations
   b. Network management
   c. Help desk functions
2. Candidates for situationally successful outsourcing
   a. Payroll systems
   b. Personnel systems
   c. Benefits systems
3. Candidates for (almost) assured failure
   a. On-line reservations systems for travel industries
   b. Deposit systems for banks
   c. Loan/sales systems for financial companies
   d. MRP systems for manufacturers

Stated another way, outsourcing candidates can be grouped into three areas: pure support functions and systems, back-office systems, and company lifeblood systems.

What Is Insourcing?

Insourcing is simple. It is the return of MIS functionality to the company or departmental environment. Just as outsourcing removes resources and personnel from an organization, insourcing increases the amount of resources and personnel in an organization. More specifically, insourcing means bringing both the responsibility and wherewithal of some part of MIS functionality back into an organization.

The impact of insourcing is that costs and responsibility are now associated directly with an internal management team. With outsourcing, internal management is placed in a passive role of providing MIS service. Thus insourcing leads to direct accountability, while outsourcing hides the accountability.

One can draw several conclusions about the management skills of a company involved in outsourcing or insourcing. Companies involved in outsourcing can easily be accused of having passive management with one possible exception. Sometimes outsourcing involves the infusion of massive amounts of capital, and there are times when the management team is able to leverage this infusion of funds into a highly profitable endeavor. In addition, major development projects can benefit from an outsourcing effort by allaying the need to allocate additional facilities and hardware resources to support supplemental labor. Insourcing, on the other hand, can be seen to indicate that upper management believes in aggressively controlling its own destiny (which is usually a good sign).

> ## Insourcing Means the Outsourcer Has *Lost* Its Job.

A Brief History of Outsourcing

Anyone looking at outsourcing as a viable option for a company must look at the steps and names associated with outsourcing before it reached its current peak of popularity. Its history is short, as befits the life span of the industry. Outsourcing started life as facilities management, which then went through the service bureau stage and emerged in its current state. The way in which it stayed alive says a lot about what its future will bring.

Facilities management came about in the mid-1960s as a cost-effective method of providing MIS services to midsize companies. The typical scenario was as follows. Computer equipment was bundled with software and was not in a competitive environment. The computer companies held all the cards in the game of supply and demand. As such, creating and maintaining a data center was an expensive proposition. Economies of scale were not just apparent, but real. Thus, large users of computer resources—big banks, aerospace companies, and others—had lots of capacity, some of which was unused.

Smaller companies were finding that maintaining a data center was more costly than they could afford, so a market for excess computer power developed. The large companies successfully marketed themselves as computer operations companies that could handle a small business along with its own. But, a funny thing happened on the way to the bank. First, it turned out to be virtually impossible for the large data centers to satisfy their outside clients. The service level of the facilities management companies always seemed to be falling. Second, computer equipment began to get cheaper, and the larger computer users had less and less advantage in procuring cheap computer power.

Three other things of significance happened in the late 1960s and early 1970s. First, IBM, one of the biggest players in facilities management, left the service bureau business. It did not leave voluntarily but was forced out of the business by an antitrust lawsuit filed against it by CDC. Second, a nationwide recession struck, which heavily impacted the aerospace and banking industries. Those companies that had large surpluses of computer power were forced to get rid of it. Finally, with the development of semiconductor memory and the introduction of *real* small-business computers, called minicomputers, the small to midsize companies could afford to acquire their own equipment.

> ## Facilities Management Failed as a Viable Service Because It Provided Little, if Any, Extra Value.

Subsequently, those noncaptive facilities management companies simply converted to service bureaus, while those captive facilities management companies left the business.

Even with the reduction in equipment costs, many smaller firms still found it beneficial to rent rather than buy. These firms bought computer time from the service bureaus that survived, or were reborn, out of the failing facilities management market. Service bureaus were never very profitable, and as the 1980s unrolled, they soon found themselves under attack on three fronts. The first front was cheaper mainframe power. The second front was increasingly powerful minicomputers. The third front was the newly created personal computer. The late 1980s saw the consolidation of the service bureau industry as more and more service bureaus became unprofitable.

The Contemporary Environment

Today's environment has a lot of similarities with the late 1960s and early 1970s. Computer technology is changing at a rapid pace, especially in the price of power. Software costs are dropping dramatically. Environmental requirements are being tremendously reduced. The bottom line of this change in technology is that there is no longer much economy of scale in computer power alone. This change in technology needs to be addressed when outsourcing is being considered.

Computer power has been dramatically reduced in cost over the last twenty years. However, MIS has not been in a position to explicitly pass these savings on to their companies. Instead, what has happened is that the amount of service MIS provides has increased. (One problem with this increase is that it has not been marketed properly to upper management, so upper management is not aware of its value.) In addition to the increased service is the fact that non-MIS areas have been increasing their local computer power through the acquisition of PCs and LANs, thus diluting the control of MIS over the computer resources.

With this decreased cost of computing power, facilities management no longer made sense. It is easy to come to the conclusion that the term *outsourcing* and the expansion of its definition were necessary tactics in order to market outside computer services to a company that already had its own MIS resources.

Outsourcing to Other Countries

It is interesting to note that India is now emerging as a major player in the outsourcing arena. During the early 1970s, India established an isolationist policy and exiled all multinational companies, including IBM, UNIVAC, and other major European and U.S. companies. However, the need for information technologies did not diminish.

Most industrialized countries have made the transition to an information technology culture over a span of forty years. In India and other third-world countries, there has been no industrial age and therefore no infrastructure to support an industrial society. Instead, these cultures have leaped from an agrarian culture straight to an information technology culture.

Several individuals in these countries recognized the opportunity to excel in information technology and developed an infrastructure to support it. India, for example, has set world records in the training of programmers with knowledge of fundamental mainframe and some middleware languages. The skill set is sufficient to accommodate any construction and unit test phase in a development effort, and the labor is cheaper than European and U.S. resources.

These "offshore" outsourcing companies have focused on building an infrastructure that supports linking via satellite to client mainframe resources, thus allaying the overhead costs of expensive mainframe hardware and adding an additional edge to the cost benefit of outsourcing. In addition, they have developed infrastructures to support the new client/server technologies.

Individual Project Tasks Are Being Outsourced.

The benefits of using offshore resources during the construction and unit test phase of a development effort are:

1. Allaying costs for additional facilities and hardware to support in-house supplemental labor.
2. Use of system resources during the client's off-hours, thus creating a 24-hour development shop.
3. Releasing key personnel to support other value-added work, such as the reconnaissance, analysis, and high level design for other projects.

While all of these make for a compelling cost benefit, it should be noted that a serious mistake often occurs during these two phases (construction and unit test) in an outsourcing effort. The mistake is underestimating the amount of resources required to support the outsourcing effort. Issues will arise during the construction period, whether in-house or outsourced, which require support from the designers and analysts. Some portion of the resources must be dedicated to resolving the issues that arise during the construction effort. The second occurrence of underestimating the resource requirements is during the acceptance of code phase from the outsourcer. Again, dedicated resources must be available to support the acceptance effort.

The Future of Outsourcing

Even though a new industry has developed around outsourcing, it looks like it will die the same death as facilities management, and for many of the same reasons. Consider the following. Facilities management companies needed a large investment in computer equipment and software. Outsourcers need a large investment in computer equipment. Facilities management companies were not able to maintain satisfying service levels. Outsourcers are facing the same problem today. (Note: Indian companies are trying not to buy their own computer power. They are selling the fact that they can utilize their clients' machines during their off-prime hours.) Computer equipment was spiraling down in cost in the early 1970s. Computer equipment is spiraling down in cost today. Outsourcers will be left holding the bag on large amounts of expensive and somewhat obsolete computer equipment in a few years, just as the facilities management companies were twenty-five years ago. The computing paradigm is changing once again. Twenty-five years ago it was going from batch to on-line. Today it is going from on-line to workstation, implying that the outsourcers are about to get caught with the wrong equipment mix. Finally, with outsourcing including systems development and maintenance, there is the added issue of a changing development paradigm. Where twenty-five years ago the change was from flat files to databases, today the change is from procedural languages to object orientation and rapid development.

Outsourcing = Facilities Management

Each of these factors reduces the value that the outsourcer can provide as the next ten years go by. In fact, each of them causes the outsourcer to be locked into obsoleting technology. The bigger the outsourcer, the more susceptible it is to this problem. Thus, if one were to take a quick look at the future, it is probable that many companies will adopt an outsourcing strategy simply to ride out the next five to ten years of technology and paradigm changes (Figure 1-1). It seems certain that many of the outsourcers are going to go out of business during those years, and the smart outsourcee should be ready to jump to insourcing before it is damaged by the change.

Those who believe that there are significant differences between outsourcing and facilities management need only to read the definition of facilities management included in *A Dictionary of Information Technology and Computer Science,* Tony Gunton, Penguin Books Limited, Oxford, England, 1990:

> **Facilities Management.** A service where the supplier takes complete responsibility for running an organization's computer systems, including developing and maintaining the applications programs, operating the machines, and dealing with the end-users.

Defining MIS

For the purposes of this book, *MIS* encompasses the entire spectrum of computer-related organizations. This definition includes computer operations, applications development, and ongoing maintenance. It also includes equipment and personnel, both operators, technical support, and programmers, which exist in end-user departments instead of the traditional data processing departments. While this definition may seem overly broad at first glance, it makes sense when these *outside MIS environments* are looked at objectively.

MIS traditionally consists of computer operations and applications development. These two organizations have the fol-

Figure 1-1. Uncertainty of future.

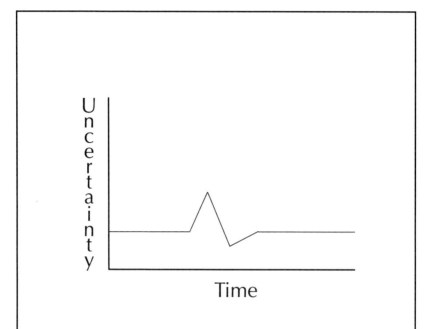

This diagram indicates changes in uncertainty over time. There is a normal level of uncertainty associated with any time span. Within that span there can be fluctuations. Depending on the size of these fluctuations, it might be advantageous for a company to outsource its MIS functions. If the level of uncertainty is very high, it might also be advantageous to outsource other company functions.

Uncertainty could be related to technology, politics, tax law, or inflation. Or it could be associated with wartime circumstances. The reason for the uncertainty may be important, or one might simply take the stance that regardless of the reason, stability is always more important.

Outsourcing could be used to reduce the risk associated with times of high uncertainty.

lowing attributes in common. First, they both require highly skilled personnel. Second, they both deal with expensive and complicated equipment. Third, the personnel in these areas are better paid than most of the other personnel in the company. Fourth, these people are important in both day-to-day operations and in preparing for the future.

When *computer* people in non-MIS departments are viewed, it becomes obvious that their attributes are the same as those in MIS. So, just as a company will look at MIS with an eye to outsourcing, it will also look to these computer people in the other departments. The success the company has in identifying these people as MIS personnel depends only on their visibility. The more visible they are, the more they are considered MIS. The executives of many user departments understand this more than most traditional MIS managers and thus try not to let their MIS personnel become too visible.

Nevertheless, MIS functions and personnel, wherever they may be and whatever they may be called, are subject to outsourcing. MIS functions in the smaller departments might be the first to be outsourced, simply because the expenses associated with them are out of line with the personnel and equipment costs of the rest of the department and are therefore very visible.

2

The Outsourcing

Outsourcing involves moving the MIS function outside the corporate structure and placing it in the hands of a service organization. It can be implemented as a partial move, as in outsourcing only the operations portion of MIS, or completely, by outsourcing both the operations and programming portions. It can even be implemented in gradations within the two types. Some companies have outsourced every portion except a single project team; others have kept a maintenance or other team together.

Outsourcing involves two companies: the client company and the outsource company. The client company is removing MIS functionality from its organization. The outsourcer is adding MIS functionality to its organization.

To begin the outsourcing, a contract is negotiated between the two. The terms of the contract vary from outsource to outsource, but they always address the following areas.

1. Initial duration of the contract. How long this agreement will be in force.
2. Terms and amounts of payments, including who pays whom, what, and when, throughout the entire duration of the contract.
3. Level of service to be received by the client company. This describes in detail how the outsourcer will keep the client happy.
4. Termination of the contract. It is fair to say that this clause all by itself will determine the feasibility or necessity for insourcing.

Once the contract has been agreed to, the real work begins. The client and outsourcer begin the implementation of the terms. The outsourcer gets to provide a valuable service to the client and receive reasonable compensation for such service. The client gets to remove the MIS function from the company structure and receive the benefit of a stable cost for those services over a set period of time.

This is a win-win situation. Both companies benefit; there really are no losers. A step-by-step look at the process of outsourcing follows.

Reviewing the Decision

How does a company come to the decision to outsource? In fact, how does outsourcing even make it into the list of options under consideration? Outsourcing is such a major step that there has to be a long-standing justification for considering it. Given the size of most MIS budgets, the normal backlog of projects, and the propensity of most projects to be brought in over budget and late, it is easy to see that a long-standing justification could be present. Other justifications for outsourcing include making the company balance sheet appear healthier, consolidating diverse operating environments, and removing incompetent managers.

> ### First and Foremost, MIS Must Realize That It Has Very Little Say in the Decision to Outsource.

Whether outsourcing is appropriate for a company depends on the finances of the outsourcing agreement, on whether an appropriate level of service can be expected from the outsourcer, and on whether the client is compatible with outsourcing.

Once outsourcing is an option, it is considered on the same basis as the other alternatives. Generally the questions most commonly asked concern the following:

- ❖ Saving money or controlling costs
- ❖ Level of service
- ❖ Compatibility with the company structure
- ❖ Management incentives
- ❖ Ability to survive the outsource effort

❖ *Is outsourcing a reaction to static or falling budgets?* Maybe the reason for the fallen service level is the budget level. If the budget was static or decreasing, it is very difficult to maintain a given service level. Even worse, it is hard to see the effect on the service level that a static budget causes (Figure 2-1). Can the outsourcer be expected to provide a better service level with a given budget level?

❖ *Can outsourcing save the client money?* On a strict dollars-and-cents level, outsourcing almost never saves the company money. But it can. The costs of some MIS functions are totally out of control and unpredictable. In these cases, an outsourcing agreement will control the costs and probably reduce them over the long run. In this situation, outsourcing can be considered the only way to control the MIS functions.

Outsourcing Probably Will Not Save Money.

❖ *Can outsourcing provide a higher level of service than can be attained with an internal MIS function?* Some MIS functions are a mess. Their processing environment is always backed up, their

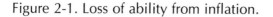

Figure 2-1. Loss of ability from inflation.

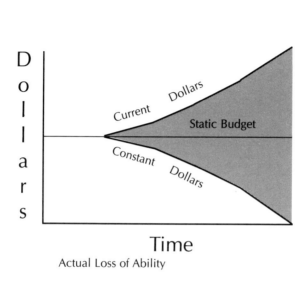

Many MIS organizations experience a static budget over the years. In some instances their budget is shrinking. The user sees this static or loss in budget monies as a reduction in service levels.

Many times upper management fools itself into thinking that processes are going just as smoothly without the extra money as with it. But just as with building maintenance or street mainte-nance, you can be sure that the loss of budget monies are causing some aspect of the functionality to deteriorate.

While other departments may refuse to accept that a static budget has an impact, the above diagram highlights what actually hap-pens. The loss of spending power is the area between the static budget and current dollars lines. The perceived loss is the area be-tween the static budget and the current dollars. The actual loss is the area between the constant dollars and the current dollars.

mess. Their processing environment is always backed up, their costs always exceed the budget, and their record of on-time delivery of development projects is disastrous. In this environment it is frustrating just waiting for normal processing to complete, impossible to plan for growth, and impossible to attain a given level of service.

With outsourcing in place, a stable level of service can be expected, because the MIS function will be operating under several important constraints. The first of these constraints deals with the rate of change within the MIS function. The outsourcer will be more prepared for the addition of new function or changes in old functions, because these items will be spelled out in the contract. In other words, the process of outsourcing will require MIS to plan ahead, which by itself will improve the service being provided.

A second reason that outsourcing can be seen to smooth service levels is that the outsourcer will always have excess capacity available. Outsourcers need excess capacity to ensure they can meet their obligations. They know that clients often understate needs, so they factor this into their environmental capacities.

❖ *Is outsourcing compatible with the company structure?* Before answering that question it is important to review the three types of MIS products. First are the back-office support products. These are the systems that perform the normal accounting functions found in every company. Examples of these are personnel, payroll, benefits, and other accounting systems. Second are the management support products. These are usually reporting and tracking systems, possibly with some executive information systems thrown in for good measure. Third are the business-specific products. These are value-added systems that transform the company product line into viable products. Examples of these are reservation systems for travel-related companies, and claims processing systems for insurance companies.

Outsourcing typically does not have a negative impact on the first two types of MIS products, back-office and staff support products. It can be devastating for the third type, business-specific products. A company must be very sure of itself before it proceeds with outsourcing this last category. This is where adequate and intelligent analysis becomes paramount. For some companies these business-specific products only make business a little easier. They are comforts, so to speak. In other companies these systems are the lifeblood of the company, and if they are hard to change or inaccessible, it could mean the death of the company. For some of these latter companies, the products are too complicated to develop themselves, so they must depend on the outsourcer.

Outsourcing Is Not Always Compatible With the Environment.

❖ *Do management incentives play a part in outsourcing?* One final but rarely discussed reason for outsourcing may have to do with management incentives. Some management teams are on short-term bonus plans, and they can increase their take-home pay simply by playing with the variables in their bonus plan formulas. One classic example of this is the return on assets (ROA) formula, which can be easily manipulated through a simple lease-back outsourcing agreement.

❖ *Can the company survive the outsourcing effort?* One very important consideration that must be recognized during the period preceding the signing of an outsourcing contract is employee morale. As soon as outsourcing becomes a consideration within the company, all MIS employees have been put on notice that they are expendable. Employee morale will drop through the basement faster than a camel can spit. MIS will be mired in uncertainty, and key personnel can be expected to leave, regardless of whether outsourcing is accepted or rejected.

> "The nature of man is such that people consider themselves put under an obligation as much by the benefits they confer as by those they receive."
> From *The Prince* by Machiavelli

Initiating an effort to look at outsourcing tells key employees two things. First, their future benefits are in doubt. Second, the company has no appreciation for the *benefits they confer.* While many employees will take a chance on future benefits, very few will stay with a company that does not appreciate their efforts.

The Balance Sheet

Regardless of the motive to outsource, there are financial implications. There are either cost savings, break-even, or avoided costs. What is certain is that MIS must identify the financial implications and present them in a financial statement. However, before MIS can address the costs, the costs must be defined. The costs identified in this effort will be based on both fact and fiction. Many numbers will be pulled out of the air. Unless MIS is diligent in developing metrics and tracking costs based on metrics, the process and its results will look like a magic trick. See Figure 2-2 for a discussion of uncertainty in spending.

There are various financial models that can be employed to determine if outsourcing is the best decision. However, the Net Present Value model, or NPV, is considered the best model. This model defines the benefit accrued over the term of a contract or

Figure 2-2. Uncertainty in spending.

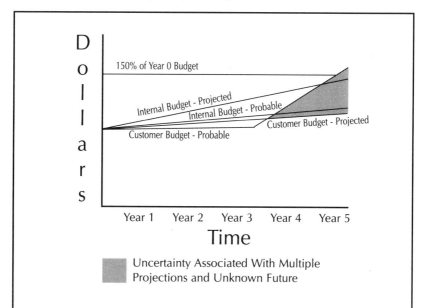

When spending projections are being made, it is imperative that the recipients of the projections remember the context in which they are given. This diagram shows five of the different factors that are involved in a normal outsourcing projection. The two most common factors are the projected costs for the in-house MIS department and the outsourcer. The next two factors are rarely considered; they are the probable costs. Note that there is a difference between projected and probable, not just in this diagram but in real life. Using the internal MIS function as an example, most companies could easily determine a probable cost if they reviewed the projected versus actual budget amounts for the last five years.

The probable costs for the outsourcer are harder to determine. The outsourcer could do the same analysis over the last five years using actual revenues. But there are two reasons why the client might not profit from this analysis. First, the outsourcer might not have been in the outsourcing business five years ago. Second, it is unlikely that the outsourcer would share its revenue history with a client.

the life of a product. Therefore, the benefits of outsourcing over the term of the contract must be measured against the cost of continuing to provide the same service in-house. In order to decide in favor of outsourcing using the NPV model, the financial benefits from outsourcing must be greater than keeping the services in-house. If they are not, the company will either break even on the outsourcing or lose money. Presumably a threshold was defined regarding expected savings and levels of services from which a decision can be made.

Remember—Just Because You Calculated the NPV Does Not Mean That You Have a *Valid* Value.

Identifying the NPV of outsourcing is important if the driving force to outsource is reducing costs. However, even if other objectives are the determinant, the NPV is still important for controlling costs during the outsourcing. Since the use of a financial model for identifying the cost of outsourcing is only as valid as the data used, the costs upon which it is based must be fairly accurate.

❖ *How are the costs traditionally identified?* If a manufacturer has a fully automated production line, specific costs are associated with an end product, and this defines a baseline. The baseline is then used in tracking costs associated with failures in the production line and cost savings or avoided costs associated with process improvements. While not all processes are fully automated, a baseline can be established where a production line-like environment exists, that is, where a series of tasks are performed in a specific sequence to complete a process. The process is executed in the same sequence over and over again. Costs are identified with the process based on time and level of proficiency, and this becomes the baseline. Individuals with little or no training are measured against the baseline to identify the delta between entry level and proficiency. Within these boundaries, performance problems are identified and costs are associated with inefficiencies.

❖ *How are baselines established in environments without repetitive tasks?* During the software development cycle the time and proficiency can vary significantly for each phase depending on the scope, that is, maintenance versus enhancements versus new development. The skill set of the individual performing the tasks can also vary significantly. As stated in the previous paragraph, the baseline must still be identified. This involves keeping track of the time and skill set of everyone involved in a project. Even if the baseline is based on a subjective best guess, it still has value. Use it, then modify it as more accurate data is obtained. Some key indicators of skill set are the thoroughness of the analysis and the number and type of defects identified during testing and in production. If defects are not tracked, then the Client Minutes of Interruption, or CMI, resulting from a production problem is an indicator of the skill set. The tracking of defects by type and severity and CMI is an accurate indicator of the efficiency of the applications developed within MIS. Costs can be associated with any of these indicators as a start in establishing a baseline.

❖ *What happens when the true cost of doing business is unknown?* At best, budgets are based on the previous year. Budgets are cut or increased without measurable indicators of spending trends. The lack of cost metrics decreases the opportunity for improving efficiency or reducing costs where needed rather than as an arbitrary percentage reduction in budget.

Costs Must Be Objective, Preferably Based on Some Kind of Metric.

A cost tracking system based on metrics enables MIS to demonstrate to the company whether it will break even with an outsourced effort or incur an increase in cost. Knowing where the money is spent also puts the MIS department in control of the budgeting cycle and minimizes the probability of outsourcing.

Making the Conversion

Converting to the outsourcer is a tedious and hair-raising process. On one hand, it may only be the movement of systems and software to a new processing platform. On the other hand, it may be all of that, plus the transfer of the MIS staff onto the outsourcer's payroll. Regardless of the extent of the outsourcing, moving systems is where existing problems are uncovered, usually the hard way.

When staff is transferred to the outsourcer, there are additional problems. Transferred staff become less and less available to the client as the conversion continues on. Combining this with the staff's unfamiliarity with the outsourcer's environment will lead to a series of problems, both large and small.

The first stage in the conversion is the planning process which addresses two areas: MIS and the user organizations. The planning process for MIS involves identifying every item within MIS to be transferred and specifying the transfer process. Items range from simple batch systems utilizing one or two tape drives or disk files all the way up to complete communications networks. Items that might be easily overlooked are the support utilities the existing facility uses, such as the specific type of sort product, and, of course, such items as the security package, or DASD, management system in place.

The planning process will also identify lead times. Although a new processor can be installed in a weekend, most things cannot be accomplished so quickly. The outsourcer will typically have to order and install additional DASD. When networks are involved, alternate communications lines need to be ordered and installed, new front ends acquired, software gens made, and so on.

The second stage involves moving software, hardware, and personnel over to the outsourcer. This will be anticlimactic if the planning stage was adequately performed. As each item is moved, a set of structured tests should be executed to verify its completeness. Once all items have been transferred, complete checks need to be performed verifying that all systems are present and interfacing with each other correctly.

The third stage involves cutting over from the client MIS to the outsourcer facilities. This process will entail several months, even if the actual switch-over is complete in one move. This is because there will be hundreds of minor details left to be resolved. Some are as simple as new report distribution procedures, others as complicated as utilizing different hardware or software procedures. As time goes by, each of the outstanding problem areas will be addressed, and within six to nine months the service level provided by the outsourcer will probably exceed that of the previous MIS function.

The transition to an outsourcer arrangement is also a significant event for the client organization. The planning process for the client involves identifying the differences between working directly with MIS and working with the outsourcer. Four major events will occur in working with the outsourcer. First, the outsourcer will take inventory of all application-related work, backlogs, work in progress, planned enhancements, and new development. What may be uncovered is application-related work being performed within the client organization because the client knew MIS did not have resources or time to do the work. Therefore, the client organization has hired some level of MIS staff to meet additional needs. The second event is the outsourcer insisting on one funnel for prioritization of work from each client department. Otherwise, there is no accurate means of identifying whether service levels are being met. This will impose a rigor on the client organizations which at best were quasi-functional in working directly with MIS.

The third event will occur after the outsourcer is doing the MIS work. That is, any changes to requirements will incur additional charges. This will impose a rigor on the client organizations to do complete analysis and provide thorough requirements to the outsourcer. This is not to say that requirements must never change during development; it is merely a wake-up call to the client organizations that business will not be conducted as usual.

The implication of these events may require a change in existing processes, or the introduction of new processes with defined roles and responsibilities.

The fourth event is the client organization actively participating in defining the service levels. For the most part the client organization has relied on MIS to determine what is best for it. This is the client's opportunity to define requirements for system availability, response time, client minutes of interruption, timely delivery of products and services, and, most importantly, measures for demonstrating improvement and efficiencies. The client organization must take full advantage of this opportunity.

Staff Reductions

Outsourcing invariably involves staff reductions. The extent of these reductions is dependent on the level of outsourcing taking place. Outsourcing only the operations area means that some existing operations staff will be transferred to the outsourcer, and some will be terminated. Outsourcing the entire MIS function is almost the same: Some will be transferred to the outsourcer, and some will be terminated. Some will remain with the client to act as liaisons between the outsourcer and the user community. Intermediate levels of outsourcing will entail varying levels of staff transfer and termination.

The effects of these staff reductions are twofold. The first is in the financial area. The company payroll and benefit costs will immediately shrink. The second is in the organizational level. The day-to-day interaction of the MIS function with the user community will cease to exist and will be replaced by a contractual relationship, just as with any other vendor.

The decrease in payroll and benefit costs will show up as an increase in efficiency or productivity of the average employee.

This is simply because the costs will no longer show up on the operating budget. The costs have not disappeared; they have been transferred to another budget item. Even so, they will have a positive impact on future costs, such as pensions.

What is immediately noticeable about the new contractual relationship between the outsourcer and the client is that it is not the same as before. This is so obvious that it is almost invariably overlooked at the real, day-to-day level. How can this be true? A quick review of the outsourcing agreement and studies will show that this was mentioned and analyzed several times. Even so, the fact remains that this is an area that can never be fully realized on an intellectual level. It is only realized upon implementation.

Informal Communication Channels Will Be Destroyed.

What most organizations overlook is that even though their organization charts show separate and distinct departments, each controlling its own destiny, this is not the reality. In the case of MIS and every other function within the company, there are two lines of communication with the user community. The first and official communication line is down through the organizational levels, from the top to the bottom. The second communication line is laterally from the user community to a lower MIS level and then back up.

This second, lateral line of communication is what makes an organization run smoothly. It is also the primary conduit for passing information about the adequacy of the current service level.

Once outsourcing takes place, this lateral line of communication is severed. It takes a while for the client to realize that it is gone, and during that time it should become apparent that the service level cannot be maintained without some sort of substitute. This substitute line of communication must be developed or the outsourcing arrangement will fail.

It is the responsibility of the client and the outsourcer to assist in the creation of these lateral, or equivalent, lines of communication.

The staff reductions bring financial benefit to the client. The movement of staff away from the user community has risk associated with it. Opportunities and risk need to be watched.

Facilities Reductions

This is the easiest area to address. Clients who outsource end up with excess facilities. Many times the outsourcer acquires the processing facilities, minus the actual buildings themselves, as part of the agreement. This is the one area in which the client always wins.

Many of the reasons supporting a client's outsourcing drive are associated with processing costs, processing capacities, and facilities costs. Many clients review their forecasted capacity requirements and wonder whether they can afford to acquire the capacity. This increased capacity often requires additional facilities space, along with added processing costs.

The one thing outsourcers can always provide is cheaper processing capacity. They can charge less for processor capacity because of the usual economies of scale. And they would not be soliciting the client's business if they could not make a profit on it while charging the same as, or less than, what the client is currently paying.

The client can be quickly rid of the facilities. The outsourcing plan is usually designed to remove the processor and peripherals as soon as possible.

One additional note: The software license fees associated with each processor can be quite substantial. These fees can be discontinued as soon as the software is no longer needed, which could be long before the physical devices are removed. However, software companies have realized that outsourcing is consolidating some of the licenses, so they are modifying their contracts to protect their revenue. Thus, reduced licensing fees cannot be considered to be a permanent attribute of outsourcing.

Temporary Increase in Consulting Fees

The client's MIS function does not always have enough extra capacity or expertise to negotiate, plan, and execute the outsourcing agreement. It is not unusual to engage a consulting firm to assist in this effort. Additional consultants may be needed to assist MIS in the normal day-to-day efforts so that the expertise within MIS can be utilized during the outsourcing conversion.

Neither of these categories of consulting costs is trivial. The consulting firm assisting in the outsourcing project can be expected to be more expensive than normal. The consultants freeing up MIS staff will be normally priced, but they may need to be available for long hours and over an extended period of time.

Although these are advertised to the client's management as one-time costs, they must still be scrutinized. On one hand, these costs must not be so great that they impact the profitability of the outsource. On the other hand, if they are not large enough, the client must be suspicious that the product being supplied is not adequate.

Both the consulting firm and the contracted replacement workers must be managed more thoroughly than any others MIS has previously engaged. If this job is not done properly, the beginning of the outsourcing arrangement will be painful and incomplete, and the client may never fully recover from it.

Immediate Effects

As a result of the excess capacity of the outsourcer, all of the production processing will be quicker. The on-line systems will experience phenomenal response time improvements. Reports will be lost in the new distribution system. Problem resolution for user-based physical problems will take longer. Bug fixes and change requests will continue as usual.

All processes that depend solely on hardware will improve. This is because of the excess capacity provided by the outsourcer. Typically the outsourcer's processors are much faster than the client's were. Even if they are not, the outsourcer probably has more of them. If the outsourcer did not have faster processors or more of them, the client probably would not have outsourced.

On-line systems respond to processing power and network design. The network installed by the outsourcer will be at least as efficient as the client's previous network. It should be more efficient and faster. After all, the outsourcer had the benefit of viewing the existing network and suggesting improvements. Upon reviewing these proposed improvements, most clients would give approval to make them.

Service and Satisfaction Will Be Better.

After outsourcing, processes that rely primarily on people will experience problems. These problems will be of the nuisance variety, but they will affect almost everyone associated with receiving or providing information manually. New procedures have to be developed. These can only take place as experience is acquired. But regardless of the experience gained, it will be impossible to totally surmount the barrier raised by the outsourcing contract. It is not possible for two companies to interface as smoothly as two functions within a single company.

It is possible that problem resolution for physical problems within the user community will take longer to be addressed, for the same reasons described immediately above. These would be both people- and procedure-related problems. They probably will never be adequately addressed, unless the client decides to handle them internally. On the other hand, if adequate service-level metrics are in place, these problems may never crop up at all.

Bug fixes and change requests will continue as usual. This will be the case even if the MIS development and maintenance staff are transferred to the outsourcer. Why is this? These processes usually were slow to begin with. If the development and maintenance staff do not transfer, there will be very little impact on the working environment except that their CPU support response times will improve. And if the staff is transferred, their new management will be making large efforts to ensure that this service is not degraded.

Technology-related processes will see a big boost. People-related processes will see a small decline. Maintenance and development processes will not be impacted. All in all, the client will be happy with the outsourcing effort. But even here it will be evident to the outside observer that most of the problems that outsourcing was to address were not addressed at the fundamental level; in fact, the fundamental reasons for outsourcing were never identified.

3

The Early Years

In the early years of an outsourcing contract, almost everything seems fine. The budgets are within the forecasts (give or take a bit), and the level of service is within tolerances. The problems that are surfacing are only those that would be expected after any type of conversion effort.

It is important to note that at this stage everyone is happy with this new relationship. The outsourcer is performing as well or better than the client's management expected. Batch processing is being completed on schedule, and the bugs are out of the report distribution and data collection procedures. The bug-reporting and -fixing procedures are working smoothly. The new projects are being integrated into the existing systems without any undue problems.

There are some clues as to the future, but nothing that any normal management team could be expected to notice, since they are not associated with problems. The first clue is that the client company has not reduced the rate at which new service requests are generated. The second is that the outsourcer is going through a few minor organizational changes to enhance its efficiency. Finally, the outsourcer is actively soliciting additional clients to use the excess processor power and programming staff it has available. New service requests mean that the client's user community wants to change with the times. Efficiency enhancements within the outsourcer mean that it is optimizing for the environment in which it is operating. Additional clients mean additional profits and a lower operating overhead *per capita* for the outsourcer.

The two expectations, new service requests and efficiency enhancements, can end up being diametrically opposed to one another. Additional clients mean that the processing windows for problem resolution are shrinking and that priority treatment of the older clients is undergoing a transformation based on the newer client's contract terms.

Moving to the Outsourcer

The move to the outsourcer is the triggering event for future insourcing. The smoothness of this move and the rapidity of deterioration of the relationship will be dependent on the degree of outsourcing taking place (operations, development, data center buyout, physical move). If a data center move is taking place, then the outsourcer will immediately be affected by all of the system support efforts that were overlooked by the client during contract negotiation. If a data center buyout is taking place (i.e., the outsourcer steps in and runs the client's data center), very few problems will be encountered. If the applications development staff is being moved, the problems will be associated with the outsourcer's standards and procedures. If a large development project is underway, large areas will be affected by the move. Problems will be encountered as each unit of work is transferred to the outsourcer. The intensity of the effort associated with resolving these problems will be dependent on the degree of outsourcing taking place.

The moving process affects the life of the contract in two ways. First, moving allows the outsourcer to judge the accuracy of the work effort involved in satisfying the basic needs of the client. Second, moving allows the client to see just how badly it has underestimated the work effort and how the outsourcer will respond to this situation. A subtle ramification of this process is that if a client/outsourcer does not go through a move, these issues will remain outstanding. (This is the situation if the data center operations are simply turned over to the outsourcer). The most likely occurrence is that the client will have underestimated the amount of work it performs, and the outsourcer will immediately have to assume a larger work load than it anticipated. This is a lose-lose situation for both parties. Consider the following scenarios.

> ## Scope of Work Misrepresentation Is the Seed of Insourcing.

Assume the outsourcer accepts the additional work effort without charge. The profits to the outsourcer are reduced. (In many cases the outsourcer is already running a deficit at the beginning of the contract.) This places the outsourcer in the position of not being able to respond to changes as time goes by. In fact, the outsourcer will probably be required to initiate premium charges soon after the conversion takes place simply to move the contract into the black. The immediate effect of this is that the outsourcer will feel that it has already done the client enough favors, and thus will take a harder line toward absorbing premium charges in the future.

Assume the outsourcer requires the client to pay premium charges for the additional work. This immediately sensitizes the client to the premium charges and causes two things to happen. First, the client's budget for the contract is already destroyed and needs to be reforecast. Second, the client is already experiencing lower than expected returns on its investment in the outsourcing agreement. The politics of this situation place the client in a tough position and will probably cause it to try to get more service from the outsourcer for the currently contracted funds. The bottom line of this is hard feelings on the part of the client.

Both parties have a vested interest in smoothing over any initial problems, such as the additional work load. The outsourcer wants to demonstrate good faith, while the client wants to save face (at least in the case of the additional work load). If one were to identify a bad guy in these circumstances, it would have to be the client. However, the outsourcer should have enough experience to understand that the client will almost always underestimate the amount of work that needs to be done. The contract signed by the two parties should have had enough monies in it to cover the additional work load. Unfortunately, outsourcers are no more all-seeing and all-knowing than the rest of us, so they often let themselves be talked into ignoring this common occurrence. The bottom line is that even though there should be no unexpected work loads, there are; and even though both parties want to get by that circumstance without prejudicing themselves or their partner, they can't.

Outsourcing contracts must be entered into only after all of the current and projected work loads are identified. Unfortunately, many clients do not do an adequate job of assessing their own requirements prior to entering these contracts.* To be successful the client must invest lots of time and effort into defining the details of the outsourced work load.

Maintaining Service Levels

Service levels are falling at an extremely slow rate. This trend will be picked up as a general feeling of dissatisfaction among the users. This trend is not being tracked by sensitive enough metrics to demonstrate it conclusively. Those falling levels that are identified are often ignored. It seems that human nature simply does not like to admit that problems exist until they can no longer be ignored. (See Figures 3-1 and 3-2.)

*Mary Lacity and Rudy Hirschheim, *Information Systems Outsourcing: Myths, Metaphors and Realities* (New York: Wiley, 1993). Three of six clients encountered major problem areas. One client was actually presented with an invoice for $500,000 from a software vendor the week it transferred to the outsourcer's data center.

Figure 3-1. Aggregate loss of service.

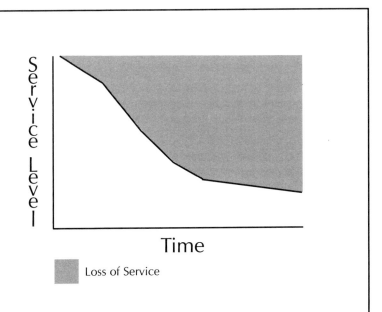

The curve in this figure shows how far the service level has dropped. If the curve is 30 percent below maximum, then the current service level is 30 percent below maximum. Using only the curve gives the *instantaneous* value of the loss. This tells only part of the story.

The aggregate loss of service is shown in the shaded area of the figure. This area represents the amount of service that has been forgone. This area could be viewed in many different ways. It could be viewed as the loss of revenue incurred through lower service levels, the loss of work performed because of lower service levels, or the amount of customer goodwill lost because of lower service levels.

The shaded area also represents the amount of money, work, or goodwill that needs to be recovered in order to bring everything back up to the 100 percent level.

Figure 3-2. Cost to repair lost service.

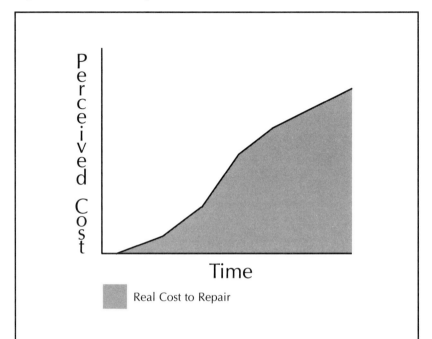

This figure shows the amount of monies needed to repair the loss shown in Figure 3-1. The shaded area under the curve represents the total amount of money. The danger of reading only the curve is that it represents the *instantaneous* cost of fixing the problem and does not address the erosion of the infrastructure implied by the loss of service over a period of time.

An additional consideration is the cooked frog effect. This is where the change is so gradual that a frog sitting in a pot of water over a fire does not realize that he is being cooked alive. Ignore the area under the curve and you ignore the damage done during the times running up to that point on the curve. The result of this is that even if the service level is down only 10 or 20 percent, the damage done may be irreversible.

This trend of falling service levels could be tracked and identified if the client and outsourcer have enough foresight and spend enough effort to develop service-level metrics. Service-level metrics are charts, figures, and information-collecting techniques that show the service level. Some of these everybody already uses, such as on-line response time charts and batch job on-time completion statistics. Unfortunately, these are not sensitive enough when used in a casual manner; it is too easy to explain away the slow rate of decline.

What is needed are additional tracking aids; for example, a combined service-level metric that can use information from all of the existing metrics and give a single number. If this metric uses all of the traditional methods, combined with new ones such as monthly surveys of user satisfaction, there is a chance that the service-level drop can be noticed and corrected. It is extremely important to recognize slowly falling service levels, because once a sizable drop in the service level is officially acknowledged, it is almost impossible for the outsourcer to get back into completely good graces with the client. *But if small drops in service level can be tracked and addressed as they occur, it is more likely that the service level will increase instead of decrease.*

Falling Service Levels Must Be Acknowledged. Sometimes Upper Management Has Too Much Ego/ Politics Riding on the Outsourcing Decision to Admit to Declining Service Levels.

Impending
Contract Negotiations

Two situations will initiate the client's consideration of renegotiating the outsourcing contract. The first is the addition of unforeseen user change requests. The second is the realization of user dissatisfaction with the service level. Unforeseen user change requests combine with the initial unidentified work load to bust the budget forecasts. These increased costs will have a tendency to erase all of the savings the client was supposed to realize from the outsourcing. Increasing user dissatisfaction is the final straw. The client will maintain that if only the user were happy, it could live with the increased expenses. This, however, is the same rationale that allowed the client to outsource in the first place.

Unforeseen user change requests will be the major impetus for renegotiating the outsourcing contract. The client will realize that the new user systems will require a larger amount of resources from the outsourcer than was anticipated. This does not mean that these resources are not available from the outsourcer. They are available, but at a cost premium over the normal services the outsourcer provides. Even though the premium was agreed to, it is not trivial, and the client only considers it as a last resort. Making the adoption of these premiums even harder is the fact that premiums are already a common occurrence. Chances are good that the client has been paying premium charges almost from the beginning of the contract. These charges would have initially been associated with the cleanup of the conversion effort. Next they would be associated with overlooked processing requirements. These premium charges have sensitized both the client and the outsourcer. The client is becoming less comfortable with the premiums, while the outsourcer is becoming more reliant on them. Eventually the client will realize that it misjudged both the amount of work and the nature of the work that needs to be performed every day.

> ## MIS Was Never Able to Forecast User Need. Therefore, They Cannot Forecast It for the Outsourcing Contract.

Most outsourcing agreements will have a mechanism in place to minimize the need for renegotiating, but this mechanism will not be adequate to support the new user change requests. Remember that the client is already paying premiums for its daily work. Obviously the terms covering additional services have already been exercised, and this situation makes it impossible to negotiate appropriate terms for the future work.

Less pressing than the user change requests will be the user dissatisfaction with the service level. Items that are individually too small to bother with will irritate the user community. The client and outsourcer will meet to address these items and to allow both sides to clear the air. To that extent the items will be addressed, but they will not be resolved. It will turn out that these are continuing items and that nothing either side does will resolve them.

> ## Users Were Never Satisfied With MIS. Therefore, They Will Not Be Satisfied With the Outsourcer.

The client will decide that all of the irritants would be resolved if the outsourcer would give the client one or more of the following.

1. A higher priority relative to the outsourcer's other clients
2. More processing capacity
3. More individual service

Of these three, receiving more individual service is the only long-term solution that will work. It is also the hardest for the outsourcer to provide. Even if the outsourcer could provide more individual service, the client/outsourcer relationship would still be suffering from the *us versus them* problem. This is where *them* is either viewed as intentionally attempting to take advantage of *us*, or *them* is simply viewed as being incapable of doing the job as well as *us*.

Eventually the client will decide that it needs to open up the contract. This is where the outsourcing agreement starts to come apart.

4

Midlife Crisis

The midlife crisis is the point at which the clues mentioned in the previous section—new service requests at the same rate as in the past, organizational changes to enhance efficiency within the out-sourcer company, continuing premium charges, and additional clients for the outsourcer—start turning into problems. There is an additional clue that is not so much the harbinger of a problem, as it is the start of a jealous relationship. Over the years the cost of technology has decreased and new technology has been introduced. Unfortunately, the cost structure built into the out-sourcing contract probably did not allow for this, and for a variety of reasons the outsourcer is not able to take advantage of this change. What is happening is that the client is starting to feel uncomfortable with the old technology, thinking that the out-sourcer is holding back on new technology for profit's sake, yet the outsourcer can't afford to make the move without an additional set of charges to the client.

Over Budget

Starting with the initial movement of resources and work from the client to the outsourcer, the client has been over budget. Several attempts have been made to move or eliminate the premium charges that are being incurred, but nothing has worked. The premium charges stem from an inadequate analysis of the requirements necessary to do the job before the outsourcing agreement was signed, all the way to the creation of new application systems for use by the client. In the beginning the outsourcer probably picked up these excess charges, but as it began to realize (or if it already realized from prior clients) that the client had continuously understated its real requirements, it was less inclined to forgive these charges. Thus the client has finally come to realize that it will always be over the forecasted budget. The most important point at this time is that the client is starting to realize that it will always understate its requirements and thus the budget it develops will always be exceeded.

The truth is that budgeting for the future is only accurate when there is no change. However, since there is always change, the future will remain unpredictable. The uncertainty associated with the future can be reduced by having extremely tight terms in an outsourcing contract. But Lacity and Hirschheim have shown that half of all outsourcing clients inadequately specify their requirements, so simply trying to build a tight contract is probably not enough. The only good solution is for the client to thoroughly investigate its requirements before the outsourcing starts. This effort will at least minimize the uncertainty involved in the contract.

Being Over Budget Is a Way of Life— No Outsourcer Can Change This.

If the client's business picks up over the life of the outsourcing contract, then its needs will increase. If the client's business remains steady during the contract life, then the service level will remain constant. The only circumstance that allows the client to escape from the over-budget condition is when the client's business goes down. If business drops, the client is definitely paying too much for the services rendered.

The bottom line is that being over budget is a way of life for the client. Whether this is bad or good depends on the size of the overrun, the reasonableness of the initial projections, and the health of the client.

Late Development

It is a fact of life that development projects typically come in late and over budget more often than not. Four out of five projects appear to come in late, have missing functionality, and are over budget. When this happens with internal projects there is some concern, but most companies seem to live with it. But when an outsourced project starts to come in late and over budget, the client is faced with real invoices for real amounts of money. The term "time is money" takes on added significance.

While it is true that there is plenty of blame to spread around for a late project, the client will almost always insist that the outsourcer absorb the extra costs. The outsourcer, on the other hand, will almost always insist that the client absorb the extra costs. The posturing by the two sides ensures that the contract will have to be renegotiated before the development efforts are complete.

Four Out of Five Projects Come in Late and Over Budget.

It does not matter who caused the development efforts to be late. This is a matter for the attorneys to discuss. The important consideration is that, 80 percent of the time, projects are late because of poorly defined requirements. In other words, the same reason for the initial premium charges is what drives the late projects. The fact is that this is entirely the fault of the client. But since the client has reduced staff as a part of implementing the outsourcing agreement, inadequate requirements are a natural side effect of an outsourcing agreement. The client is predisposed to develop incomplete requirements from the second the outsourcing agreement is signed. This reads like a Catch-22. The client can only save money by outsourcing, but when the client outsources, the requirements become incomplete, so costs go up. Add to this the fact that, regardless of the cause of the late development efforts, the client will perceive a drop in the service level. Once again it is impossible to build a winning outsourcing agreement.

Staffing Expertise

The general rule is that staff resign when an outsourcing agreement is announced. The specifics are that the most qualified and sharpest personnel resign the quickest. While most outsourcing agreements require the outsourcer to employ the client's staff for a set period after the contract start, in practice this does not happen. It is not unusual to see a staff migration of 50 percent or greater between the time the outsourcing agreement is signed and the time it takes effect. It is also not unusual to see an additional 50 percent decrease in the remaining staff by the time the employment period is finished. All told, the client can expect that 75 percent of its pre-outsourcing agreement staff will be gone by the time the outsourcer is free to terminate the client's employees.

> # Figure on Losing 75% of Staff Between Migration Start and Finish.

While many clients justify the outsourcing effort by counting the savings they get from the staff reductions, they seldom realize the value of the decline in service level that savings buys them. Unlike many other departments within a company, MIS personnel are typically not commodities. While a programmer with five or ten years of experience can be hired off the street, those equivalent years of business applications expertise cannot be hired off the street. Today, application systems are mostly custom systems, regardless of all the talk about reusable code and common platforms. This means that the client's application systems are unique and require personnel with specific knowledge for their maintenance, execution, and enhancement.

There is no way that a cut in personnel can simply result in decreased outsourcing costs. The first time specialized expertise is needed, there will be a reflection in either premium costs or reduced service levels. Once again, this leads to a Catch-22 situation. Savings from outsourcing agreements usually come from reduced head counts. But reducing head counts increases the outsourcing premium costs and decreases the perceived and actual service level.

Declining Service Levels

Before continuing, it is important to realize that the client will view maintaining the status quo as a declining service level. What this means is that as technology becomes more powerful, clients will expect that service will improve. Therefore, if the service level does not improve, the client will perceive it as having dropped. This means that the outsourcer is starting out as a failure because it believes that simply maintaining the current service level is adequate. (See Figure 4-1.)

Once the outsourcer has enhanced the efficiency of its organization to process the existing work load and added new customers, it can no longer respond to problems and service requests as quickly as in the early days of the contract. The perceived and the actual service levels are declining.

Figure 4-1. User community expectations.

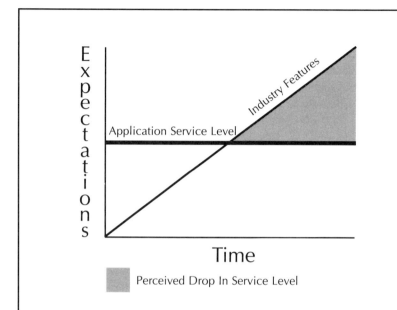

The expectations of the user community are set by the environment in which they exist. When a system is first introduced, the users are pleased. They have a system that has more features than normally available in the industry. But as time goes on, the industry features increase, and there comes a point when the industry has more and better features than the user's system.

At this point the user perceives a drop in service level. Even though nothing in the system has degraded, the features list is out of date. As far as the user community is concerned their system now has less value to them. They need additional features in order to compete or work effectively.

The problem is that since the system is no longer under development, but has entered the maintenance mode, users do not feel they need to pay much for the additional feature. The problem is compounded when MIS takes the stance that they need monies of the magnitude used in new development to add the features.

> # Constant Service Levels Will Be Perceived as Dropping Service Levels.

Some clients have the foresight to build inflation clauses into their contracts. These clauses typically require the outsourcer to increase the service level by some percentage every year in exchange for a corresponding increase in payments by the client. This is still inadequate. If the service level increases along with the compensation, the client is still not getting any more for its money. The best it gets is that the client is standing still. This is a fundamental problem with outsourcing. Costs always go up and the service level always goes down.

> # Today's Metrics Don't Provide the Information Needed to Identify and Resolve Problems.

Remember that MIS projects always come in over budget and behind schedule. The reasons for this are too numerous to recount here. This is one of the major reasons that the client outsourced in the first place. Outsourcing is an attempt to cap the cost on these projects and appears to protect them from the effects of this reality. The key word here is *appears*. Just as zero inflation cannot be legislated by fixing prices, the effects of over-budget and late projects cannot be avoided by moving those responsibilities to the outsourcer.

The outsourcer is absorbing some of the effects of these over-budget projects, and these effects are being dissipated as lower profits and increased costs. To the client this is seen as decreased flexibility in the handling of new requests. To the outsourcer this creates an increased impetus to sign up new clients. But as mentioned before, signing up new clients has the effect of decreasing the service level provided to the existing clients. It is a Catch-22 situation for the outsourcer. The outsourcer needs more money, and the only recourse open to it is the acquisition of new business, but new business will always lower the existing level of service.

Eventually the outsourcer realizes that it must renegotiate its contracts with the majority of its older clients. This is the only avenue open to it that actually allows it to increase the service level back up to acceptable norms. Unfortunately, the very act of soliciting the new funds from existing clients causes the older client's perceived service level to drop. After all, the client is paying more, but getting only the same level of service originally contracted for.

And finally, realize that any outsourcer can quit the business, voluntarily or otherwise. Several outsourcers whose primary business is not outsourcing have already left or announced their intention of leaving the field. Their clients are facing now what others might face in the future.

> ## You Cannot Legislate Either Zero Inflation or No Responsibility for Over-Budget Situations.

User Dissatisfaction

The user community within the client company believed that outsourcing would decrease the level of outstanding service requests. It also believed that the outsourcer would bring additional expertise to bear on these service requests. The client company believed that this additional expertise would bring it everything it ever wanted in an MIS organization. Unfortunately for the client, these expectations are not being met. The expectations were unreasonable to begin with—there is no silver bullet to reduce the backlog of service requests.

With the signing of the outsourcing contract, the user community has lost all of its *contacts* with the MIS department. The usual casual environment in which its priorities were addressed has been replaced by a contractual environment. Everything the community gets is specified in the contract; anything not in the contract is extra. Anything not spelled out in explicit detail in the contract is open to on-the-spot renegotiating. The negotiators are the client's user, who needs added functionality, and the outsourcer, who needs to keep costs low. It is no longer easy to shuffle personnel and resources to satisfy the user community's changing needs.

> ## Users Are Always Dissatisfied. Think of Them as Looking for Reasons to Support This Attitude.

Several other major issues enter into the picture here. The first is that the personnel employed by the outsourcer are no longer captive to the client, but are shared among all of the outsourcer's clients. The second is that there is no longer a team spirit shared between the MIS personnel and the user community. In fact, as personnel are shared among clients and the user community's dissatisfaction increases, team spirit is replaced by an adversary relationship. Communications between the user community and the outsourcer get worse, not better.

If the client's remaining MIS staff is being used as a liaison between the user community and the outsourcer, the picture is even worse. The user community must present its grievances to the MIS staff, who have no power to control the outsourcer. It is possible that the MIS staff will not even transmit the grievances correctly to the outsourcer. The user community does not even have the satisfaction of complaining to the very people supporting it. (See Figures 4-2, 4-3, and 4-4.)

Basically, the user community feels it has been had. The client company is saving money on paper, but increasing the work load on the user community. Why is it increasing the work load? Simply because the services that the user community requests from MIS always have to do with reducing work load. If the service request is not adequately addressed by MIS, it either does not reduce the work load or causes the user community an added inconvenience (adding to the user community's work load).

Reviewing Current Technology

The client's MIS staff, which no longer has to deal with day-to-day problems in the detail they used to, is now free to look at current technology. Current technology is seen in the light of what could be possible, not what is possible. The MIS staff no longer has a feel for the pain and suffering involved in bringing new technology on-line for the client. It has been years since this staff was directly involved in developing a new system or modifying an existing system to accommodate new technology. It is not good enough to watch, or liaise to, a system under development. As it is, MIS has lost the touch. It is slowly losing its expertise in analyzing the costs and difficulties of implementing service requests.

(text continues on page 54)

Figure 4-2. Internal requests for service diagram.

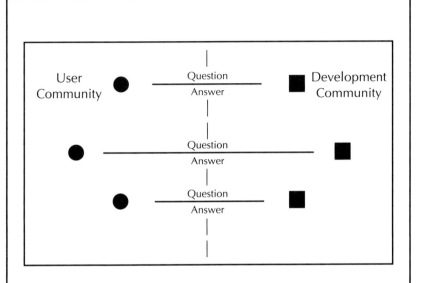

When MIS is a part of the company and the user makes requests, they are usually directed exactly to the right person and typically handled informally first, and then officially confirmed later. In theory the requests are made through formal channels, but as most employees know, this is not how it works in reality.

What really happens is that a user will require some support from MIS. This user will then call one or more people in MIS requesting assistance. When the right person is found, the user will ask if that support person is available to help. The support person says, "Sure, what do you need?" If the request is small, the support person satisfies it right there. If the request is large, the support person says, "Call my manager and tell them that I can do this but it will take x amount of my time."

In the second case, the support person then tells their manager that they talked to the user and the request is coming. In other words, all of the request overhead is already complete before the request is officially made.

Figure 4-3. External requests for service.

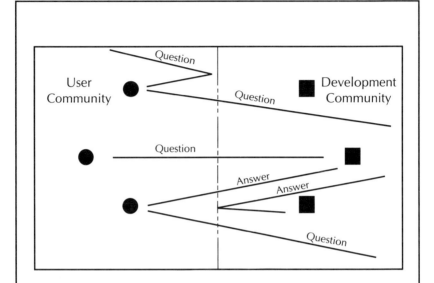

The way requests are processed changes when MIS is replaced by an outsourcer. The familiar and informal communication paths used within the client company no longer exist. As a consequence, requests for services take a more indirect and less certain routine.

A barrier exists between the user community and the outsourcer's development and operations community. Requests made by the users need to penetrate this barrier when going to the outsourcer and again when returning from the outsourcer. Several examples of stylized communication flows are shown in this figure.

Some user requests don't make it to the outsourcer because the user does not know how to navigate the bureaucracy. Other requests make it to the outsourcer, but do not get to the correct person. Some requests make it through the barrier to the correct person, only to fail to get back to the user making the request. While everyone will agree that these scenarios should not happen, in real life they always do.

Figure 4-4. External requests without answers.

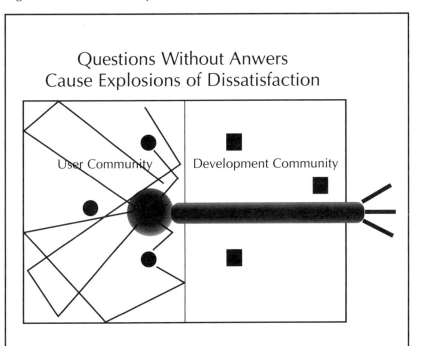

Once friction starts to occur between the client and the outsourcer, the communications paths become more formalized. The intent of the formalization is to make sure that all requests for services are handled in an expeditious fashion and that none are lost or misinterpreted. The effect of this formalization is the opposite of what was intended. As the process becomes more formalized and controlled, the amount of requests that is received by the outsourcer, acted on correctly, and returned to the user community becomes smaller and smaller.

Eventually the user's perception is that nothing is being done correctly or in a timely manner and their level of frustration increases. Once this level hits critical mass, the user community blows away the formal procedures and overwhelms the outsourcer. It is hard to imagine that any outsourcing agreements can withstand this type of pressure.

As a consequence of this, the client finds itself believing that the outsourcer is overcharging for new service requests and dragging its feet during the development efforts. Although there is some truth to both of these beliefs, they are not true enough. The MIS staff, through their lack of participation in the day-to-day development of new systems, is becoming another user community. They can no longer support the client company by keeping a close check on the outsourcer's development efforts. They will either become cheerleaders for the outsourcer's development staff or they will become a "Doubting Thomas" of everything the outsourcer attempts to do.

MIS Is Eyeing New Technology and Saying to Itself: *If Only . . .*

In either case, the stage is set for the client to start thinking about insourcing. This thinking starts with a review of today's current technology. In the first case, the user community will become disaffected with the entire process and will start looking at technological solutions to protect itself. In the second case, the MIS staff will start analyzing current technology with an eye towards insourcing. Both cases start with looking at current technology.

It goes without saying that today's technology gives more value for the dollar than yesterday's technology. It also goes without saying that the outsourcer has acquired a lot of yesterday's technology. Further, it is not easy, or sometimes even possible, for the outsourcer to upgrade enough of its existing *yesterday's technology* to current technology.

Finally, compounding all of the above obvious issues, MIS will conveniently forget the amount of effort and uncertainty associated with its own upgrade efforts. Many upgrade ventures undertaken by the previous personnel in MIS (who have almost certainly left the company by this time) suffered minor to major failures. Some of these failures probably cost the client major amounts of money and lost employee productivity. But since the client is now explicitly paying the outsourcer to perform these upgrades, problems are not tolerated. After a few of these failures on the part of the outsourcer, the client may even refuse to allow the outsourcer to upgrade to newer equipment.

Therefore, it is obvious that the client's user community or MIS staff will find that current technology can perform better than the outsourcer and at a lower price.

It is at this point that the client will start to consider insourcing as an option for the future.

5

The Insourcing

Insourcing means competing with vendors to perform MIS functions for the end user. The scope of insourcing can range from reestablishing an MIS department to simply retooling existing resources to more effectively and efficiently satisfy end-user requirements. The premise of insourcing in this section assumes the entire MIS function has been removed and a business case is required to reinstate the functionality with company resources.

While the premise focuses on building an MIS department from the ground up, the areas for consideration are applicable to any scope of insourcing.

Insourcing is an exciting and tantalizing idea. Knowledge of all the mistakes learned by the previous MIS function, which led to the outsourcing, along with all of the lessons learned from the outsourcing, make the existing MIS staff heady with anticipation. Very few MIS functions had the opportunity to be created in one fell swoop. Everyone else has been built up from existing staff, equipment, and software. This will be different. The software systems are existing, but all of the staff and equipment will be new.

This can be a dream come true, or it can be a nightmare. Data centers are not cheap, and seldom can they be designed to match a company's needs exactly. Insourcing after outsourcing presents a situation where a data center can be designed to match the company's actual needs. Staffing is important and very difficult. But the company no longer has the old personalities. It can go out and get exactly what it needs. It can hire the best and build a staff comparable to no other. Of course, the company will need the money to buy the best and astute management to recognize the best. In fact, it will need great management to recognize what is needed and then hire the best people for that need.

Insourcing is an opportunity to create the best, to start over with a clean sheet and to do it right. But insourcing is the hardest work an MIS staff will ever encounter. It is the single most expensive project ever and it will take years to complete. And it will affect every user, manager, and department in the company. Insourcing will probably also require a lot more money than anyone ever expected.

Even as the company prepares for insourcing, MIS needs to understand how the company perceives its role. If the company perceives MIS as having a different role than MIS sees itself having, there will be a constant burden to deal with.

MIS Is Not Perceived as Being a Core Function.

Most companies focus on core business functions and the need to reduce and/or off-load capital expenditures. MIS functions are rarely perceived as core business functions; they are often viewed as supportive. Therefore, support can be purchased from external providers. The amount of capital expenditures associated with MIS departments, i.e., desktop computers, computer hardware, licenses, and maintenance, can easily amount to 10 percent of all capital expenditures. Reducing MIS capital expenditures visibly adds to the profit margin. Since MIS is viewed by upper management as an area in which they can make *big* cuts, MIS must make a special effort to protect itself. Therefore, the following approaches will ensure that MIS gets the attention of the executive management and, potentially, may aid in obtaining the funds for a new MIS department.

Strategic Approach

Winning the decision to insource the MIS functions requires a strategy that demonstrates to executive management that MIS is a core function, adds value, and contributes to the profit margin in a positive way. Developing a strategy is an arduous process requiring adherence to a methodology and the commitment and discipline to see the process through to the end. In its simplest form, a strategy defines a *vision, goals* and *objectives,* and a *plan of action* that encompasses a direction for the future. MIS may consider enlisting the assistance of consultants specializing in this area of expertise. An alternative is to read through numerous published methodologies regarding the development of business strategies. Either approach is plausible; however, dedication to implementing the strategy and to continuously assessing the need for change is paramount to success. One side effect of this effort, establishing credibility with executive management, has extremely important long-term consequences.

> # The Insourcing Team Must Think Like Entrepreneurs.

Most managers are capable of operating a function of an existing business; however, few managers are entrepreneurs. Even fewer managers are capable of extending the business function by developing a long-term strategy. Personnel require entrepreneurial skills if they are to develop the strategy for a new MIS department. Entrepreneurial skills require the ability to think globally with regards to the dynamics of the political, social, and economical impacts on the business. Entrepreneurial thinkers recognize the potential impact of demographics on the labor force. An understanding of how all of these forces converge to change a business separates the entrepreneurial manager from the traditional MIS manager. It is important that the MIS management team develop these entrepreneurial skills.

The following identifies the key areas to address when developing a functional strategy. A distinction is being made between a business strategy and a functional strategy, as the premise of this book is that the MIS department is a functional department within the company in support of the core businesses. The functional strategy must align with the corporate strategy. (See Figures 5-1 and 5-2.)

Having a Strategy Demonstrates You Know Where You Want to Go.

Developing a strategy requires some up-front work. The first step is the *business analysis*. The business analysis addresses two key areas: First, the analysis determines the type of business MIS wants to be in. This may sound like a rhetorical question; however, the answer will determine the type of strategy that will be developed. For instance, if MIS wants to develop software with the intent of selling the software to make a profit, the strategy must be a marketing strategy. If the intent is to develop software for internal use, consideration must be given to how much of the development life cycle will be done in-house. Will construction and unit testing be outsourced? Is this a viable alternative to consider for keeping costs down? The second area the business analysis addresses is identifying what the MIS department will do differently from the current outsourcer; in other words, gap analysis. This strategy lies in stressing the differences between MIS and the outsourcer and how MIS will leverage the differences to the advantage of the company.

The next step towards a strategy is *organization development*. This area addresses the core competencies of your department.

(text continues on page 62)

Figure 5-1. Strategic planning model overview.

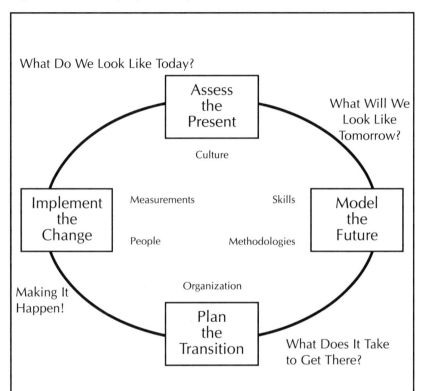

The Strategic Planning Model is a classic model for any plan to implement change. The gap analysis between the future and present identifies the areas that must be addressed for the transition. The key to this model is the transition plan. Most strategic plans fail because a transition plan is never developed. The transition plan is the road map to the future.

The strategic model encompasses the Organizational Model, which addresses the culture, measurements, skills, methodologies, and the organization. There is an interdependency between the strategic plan and organization development.

Figure 5-2. Strategic planning details.

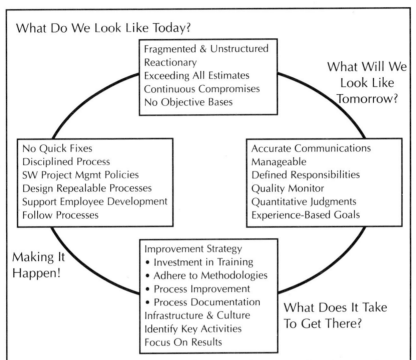

What Do We Look Like Today?

Fragmented & Unstructured
Reactionary
Exceeding All Estimates
Continuous Compromises
No Objective Bases

What Will We Look Like Tomorrow?

No Quick Fixes
Disciplined Process
SW Project Mgmt Policies
Design Repealable Processes
Support Employee Development
Follow Processes

Accurate Communications
Manageable
Defined Responsibilities
Quality Monitor
Quantitative Judgments
Experience-Based Goals

Making It Happen!

Improvement Strategy
• Investment in Training
• Adhere to Methodologies
• Process Improvement
• Process Documentation
Infrastructure & Culture
Identify Key Activities
Focus On Results

What Does It Take To Get There?

The details of the Strategic Plan provide a sample of some key areas to address for process improvement. The future should depict the idealistic environment an MIS organization wants to create. The present should be as objective as possible, with an accurate representation of the current environment. It is imperative to be as honest as possible. Be cautioned: it is easy to gloss over lack of procedures, processes, and methodologies because work is being done. However, the present sets the basis for the transition plan.

The transition plan must allow for several iterations in order to achieve the panacea. The present was not created overnight and the solution will not be accomplished overnight.

The key to the strategic plan is to identify milestones and track to the milestones, making changes as necessary in relation to the overall strategy.

What is the MIS approach to dealing with the competition? What is the competitive edge the MIS department possesses over the outsourcer? What will MIS do better than the competitor? What type of an organization will MIS have? Team work groups? A hierarchy? Will MIS conduct its development on the mainframe or use client/server? Making decisions based on the answers to the questions posed during the initial analysis shapes the vision and goals for the MIS department.

The next step is the articulation of the strategy. The strategy begins with what is known as the *mission statement*. The mission statement identifies what MIS will deliver to the client and is the concept of what the organization is to become and do. Next, identify the *objectives*. These are also referred to as key performance indicators, or KPI, and are the determinants for measuring success. Include objectives that identify strategic success and financial success. For instance, some objectives could be to reduce costs, contribute to the profit margin, improve service levels, or reduce development cycle time. Notice these are quantifiable measures. All of these decisions will ultimately influence the effectiveness of the strategy and the success or failure of the MIS department.

The final step is the development of the *strategy*. This identifies the approach you will take to meet your objectives. Will MIS leverage new technologies, such as WAN, Internet, mobile computing, or all of them? Will MIS outsource or do all of the development life cycle in-house? The *strategic plan* identifies the road map for achieving the goals and objectives. The *implementation plan* identifies roles, responsibilities, and milestones in pursuing MIS objectives. The milestones serve as the indicators for assessing the effectiveness of the strategy. They can also be used to determine the need for change if they appear to be unattainable.

Successful strategies rest on the understanding that a strategy is a long-term goal, and that the tactics that get MIS to that goal can evolve as a part of the process.

Tactical Approach

In any organization, there are political implications when requesting monies. There is an order of magnitude between the amount of monies requested and the amount of political obstacles to overcome. The following tactics will further assist in acquiring funds for the MIS venture. First, develop a partnership with the user organizations, and second, develop a business plan. Both require special skill sets: soft skills, business skills, and financial skills. Each will allay some of the political obstacles and, more importantly, gain credibility with the financial officer, who controls the money.

To define the tactics, it is imperative to review the initial justification for outsourcing the MIS functions, particularly if the same key decision makers are still in place within the organization. The probability of finding allies within the group who decided to outsource will be difficult at best, if not impossible. It is hard to admit a mistake, particularly if the decision resulted in negative cash flow. Developing an alliance with the user community is not difficult since it is living with lower service levels. The partnership with the users will allay some of the political roadblocks. The premise for the partnership must be the improvement of the service levels and the reduction of the delivery times. The partnership must also incorporate the exchange of information regarding business needs and MIS functionality.

To facilitate the partnering, the MIS personnel must view themselves as consultants to the users. Good consultants acquire business knowledge of the company through the users. This ensures that the product developed will support the end user in its interactions with the customer. Good consultants also provide knowledge to the end user regarding IT technologies, enabling the end user to assist in exploiting the technologies. By acquiring an understanding of each other's areas of responsibilities, the users develop realistic expectations of the MIS department, and MIS can better represent the users.

> **Tactics Must Always Support the Previously Developed Strategy.**

If the credibility of the MIS department was in question and was a reason for outsourcing the MIS functions, that is, the costs were out of control and product delivery was past due, then improvement in service levels through use of new technology and fewer employees will strengthen the business plan. However, improvement must be measurable. Metrics must be developed as a joint effort between the MIS and the end users, with the customer as the ultimate determinant of value added. Using the customer to measure the effectiveness of the MIS department strengthens the partnership with the end user since the end user, in turn, is measured through customer satisfaction.

A distinction must be made between a business case and a business plan. The assumption being made in this discussion is that the entire MIS department was outsourced, and therefore this is a start-up venture, from ground zero. Developing a business plan has significant implications in relation to the work required. It requires another specialty skill set rarely observed in MIS departments: finance. *MIS should seriously consider obtaining assistance from a professional when the real financial number crunching begins.*

During the exercise of developing a business plan, the MIS department will determine for itself in "red and black" whether the notion to insource justifies the cost. The following are key areas in a business plan.

❖ As with a business case, a detailed description of the purpose and services MIS will provide is necessary. This is appropriately called the *business description*.

❖ The next area to address is the *market plan*. This may appear out of context for an MIS department; however, the premise is that the MIS department is competing for a "share of the market," the share the outsourcer currently holds. The market plan identifies the services that the MIS department will provide more efficiently and at lower cost. The market plan also defines the methodology and strategy employed to compete.

❖ The *competitive analysis* process identifies the strengths and weaknesses of the competition. A strategy is identified that provides a distinctive edge over the competition. This includes the assets and skills that enable MIS to be competitive.

❖ The next two phases are often defined after the financial phase is completed. However, for presentation purposes, the financial phase is placed after the operations and management phase. The *design and development* phase of the business plan is used for designing the services or products and the goals associated with each service or product. This is where the money begins to appear. The plan identifies the costs during the development of the services and products, including hardware and software. Start-up costs can be significantly higher considering the system resources required to support the existing software plus costs for items such as hardware, licenses, and DASD.

❖ The *operations and management* phase defines the ongoing costs of operation. The organizational structure is defined during this phase, inclusive of the required skill sets to operate the department. The organizational structure is a key determinant of the budget since labor is the major monthly expenditure. The capital outlay for hardware and software must be considered in terms of depreciation and costs for licenses. A key item for identifying the scope of the money requirements is the amount of budgeted monies for MIS functions at the time of outsourcing. These monies represent the depreciation of the hardware and software and assume that changes to software and the addition of upgrades to hardware are incremental costs. Fixed expenditures are also included as part of the budget at the time the outsourcing occurred.

❖ The *financial plan* requires a sophisticated understanding of finance. The key to this phase is the details, where the number crunching begins. This is also where the MIS department makes or breaks the overall venture. The financial plan consists of the income statement, which demonstrates the projected profit and loss; the cash flow or budget, or what it takes to run the venture; and the balance sheet, a description of the assets and liabilities.

Is all of this work worthwhile and necessary? Yes. Doing this work demonstrates that the MIS department has the discipline to be successful. This work also demonstrates the capability of the MIS department to contribute to the overall economic health of the company.

Technology Review

During the years of the outsourcing agreement, technology has marched on. The equipment used by the client has been obsolete for at least one generation, and probably two. The equipment used by the outsourcer is also at least one generation old. This means that the client has the opportunity to pick up all the processing power it needs for the next five years at a very good price.

It is possible that all of the end user equipment, such as terminals and personal systems, was transferred to the outsourcer. If so, MIS must review the current end-user technology. Without a doubt, MIS can acquire considerably more power and flexibility for the end user than ever before, or MIS can adopt the same old technology at a greatly reduced price. The major consideration at this point is once again the potential user requests for technology (such as imaging systems). A decision on price alone could hobble the expansion capabilities of the company.

Traditional corporate data centers and their corresponding development organizations are based on IBM System 390 technology. The big data centers are running under MVS (and moving to OS/390), the smaller under VM and VSE. Midsize data centers are running under IBM AS/400 technologies or large UNIX or VMS machines. Small data centers are running under small IBM AS/400 technologies, small UNIX machines, or large PCs. The change in technologies in these platforms between 1990 and today is astounding.

The options available in 1990 were orders of magnitude less than today. These options have changed in both the areas of hardware and software. Today a new System 390, capable of supporting up to 200 CICS users, can be purchased for $35,000 (the supporting software would cost about $115,000). The super mainframe class machines now start at under $1,000,000, while they ran about $20,000,000 in 1990. Object-oriented languages are now available for business (including COBOL). GUI interfaces are now available for business and mainframe applications (including COBOL). Relational databases for PCs can now support millions of rows of data (DB2, ORACLE, or SYBASE, to name a few).

Production platform paradigms have also enlarged. Client/server technology has now reached the point of being accessible and inexpensive to acquire, although it is still expensive to program and maintain. MIS is no longer tied to one type of information technology. There are plenty of alternatives to review.

Waiting for New Technology Is a Losing Proposition. Never Bet on a Promised Product.

MIS can take two different approaches when considering the technology to use. These approaches depend on the technology paradigm being adopted. In the traditional arena of mainframe/large minicomputer processing, MIS can go first class with new equipment and acquire current technology immediately. This has the benefit of guaranteeing that there is enough processing and storage capacity to handle the client's needs. The second approach is to step back one generation and pick up slightly less processing power and capacity for a substantially smaller amount of money. In the PC and client/server paradigm, MIS can utilize centralized servers or distributed servers. The first case requires that the new super servers be adopted, thus providing MIS with the most up-to-date technology. The second case allows MIS to pick up midsize PCs for the local servers, thus trading lower server costs for increased maintenance costs.

The choice will usually be made based first on the financial situation of the client and second on the prejudices of the MIS management.

New technology will also be available for the network. New lines need to be ordered, and this gives the company the opportunity to increase the bandwidth of the network. This is a purely technical decision and will be made by the MIS staff. It is important that this staff consider other new technologies, such as imaging systems and the needs that they have. This means that MIS must pull out the crystal ball and assign probabilities to the types of new software and hardware technologies they will be dealing with in the years to come.

For some reason, it is harder for companies to justify an increase in network capacity than increases in DASD or processing capacity. That is why future networking usage must be forecast more correctly than the mainframe hardware.

Building the New Department

A great deal of magic is associated with the creation of an effective department. Indeed, it is almost impossible to forecast the success or failure of an organization. This uncertainty is so prevalent that many large organizations seem to be perpetually reorganizing, apparently in the hope that one day management will stumble on the right combination. Against this backdrop, it is easy to forecast that building a new department is even more difficult. For one thing, even though many managers lament the fact that they must work with the people they have, the truth is that finding people to fill open positions is even more difficult than using the people already available! Given the tenuous position MIS is in, developing a department from the ground up is a high-risk proposition. A conceptual understanding of organizational development will remove some of the magic needed to create an effective department.

Organizational Considerations

Building an organization is typically considered an art instead of a science. Ironically, organizational development employs methodologies to construct new organizations or change existing organizational structures, and the word *methodology* implies a scientific approach. The primary driving force of an organizational structure is the discipline the organization chooses to focus on, such as providing services, new product development, or operations. Answering this question is the most important task MIS must address. Commitment to only one of the disciplines will drive all subsequent actions and facilitate defining the required strategy, goals, and objectives. Some clarification is required regarding the selection of one of these disciplines. While each of these disciplines plays a role in the organization, it must be understood that choosing one discipline does not preclude a commitment in some degree to the other two disciplines. What it does mean is that all decisions are weighed against the overall objectives of the discipline selected—for instance, being a low-cost provider. This becomes the credo by which all decisions are made.

The first step is to define the work, roles, and responsibilities associated with the selected discipline. The second step addresses selecting the most appropriate organizational structure to support the discipline selected. The organization's structure could be hierarchical, cross-functional, centralized or decentralized, or a combination of these. Other considerations are (1) how will communication, processes, and system flow? and (2) what kinds of performance management and compensation should there be?

Select a Discipline, Choose an Organizational Structure, Address the People.

The third step addresses the people. What culture is most conducive to the nature of the work: authoritarian, collaborative, technical, or purposive culture (meaning the culture is driven by a purpose, usually one that will make the world a better to live)? William E. Schneider defines the different cultures in his book *The Reengineering Alternative.**

Using the organizational development methodology for defining an organization facilitates the subsequent processes of identifying roles, responsibilities, and how authority is addressed. (See Figures 5-3 and 5-4.)

A Quick Look at Organizational Structure

The most important attribute of an effective organization is that all responsibilities need to be identified and assigned to management units. The key here is that each responsibility must be assigned to one, and only one, management unit. Matrix management is a glaring example of the wrong way to assign responsibility. People with more than one boss essentially have no boss.

The second most important attribute is the assignment of authority. Managers who have a given responsibility must have the authority associated with that responsibility. In the most common case for employees assigned to a manager, the manager must have the authority to direct the actions and future of the employees. Managers who cannot hire and fire are one example of the wrong way to assign authority. Another more subtle example is salary guidelines that make it virtually impossible for a manager to reward or punish exceptional performance. Finally, in a non-personnel area, managers must have the authority to make and enforce decisions regarding their interactions with other management areas.

The next attribute of an effective organization is an unambiguous communications network. People seeking information, assistance, and services from and within the organization must

*Schneider, William E, *The Reengineering Alternative* (Burr Ridge, Ill.: Richard D. Irwin, Inc., 1994).

Figure 5-3. Organizational design model overview.

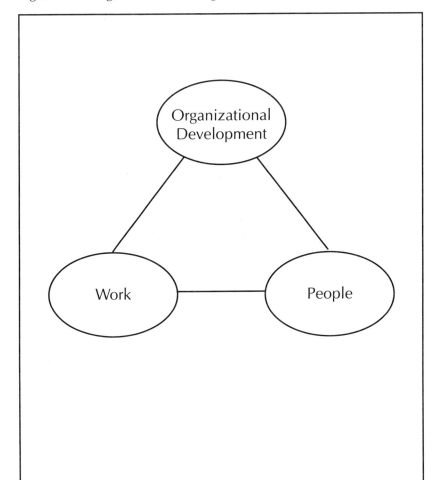

The Organizational Design Model is a model for implementing organizational effectiveness in a functional area of a business. The model identifies the interrelation among three entities of a functional area: the people, the organization, and the work.

The organizational model is interdependent with the strategic plan. The organizational model focuses on strengthening the capabilities of the organization to successfully deploy the strategic plan.

Figure 5-4. Organizational design model details.

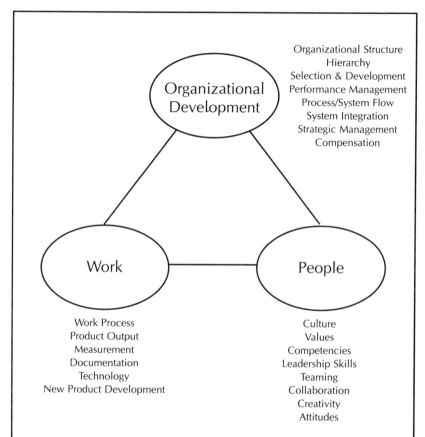

The details of the organizational design model provide a sample of some key areas to address in order to achieve organizational effectiveness. The organizational model identifies the dynamic interactions among all three entities of the model.

The organizational entity creates and fosters the environment in which the people accomplish the specified work. The work entity defines the core competencies in relation to a selected discipline. The people entities address the cultural changes and skills required to carry out a strategic plan. The interaction of the three entities creates the overall infrastructure for a functional area.

have clearly defined *single* contact points. In other words, for each management unit there must be one, and only one, contact point referenced by people outside of the management unit. The reason for this may not be clear at first, but consider the following argument. If there are two contact points within a management unit, someone from outside the organization, *someone not in the know,* has a 50 percent chance of approaching the wrong person. When they do contact the wrong person, they come away saying to themselves that they will contact the other person first the next time. As time goes on, the second contact becomes the primary contact, and her skills increase, or her work load increases, and the initial contact person starts to lose skills and work. Before long the initial contact person has no value to the management group, and, by definition, anyone who approaches him will be approaching the wrong person. The point is this: There should be one contact point per management unit. More than one person guarantees confusion and reduced service levels.

> # Responsibility, Authority, Recognition of Authority, and Unambiguous Communications Channels.

One final attribute is required in effective managers. Managers are both the regulators and the distributors of work and information. Ineffective or semi-effective managers are a bottleneck constraining the service level of an organization. If a manager is 80 percent effective instead of 100 percent, work flowing through his area will take 25 percent longer than necessary. If this seems surprising, when a manager is only 50 percent effective, work will take 100 percent longer than necessary.

Using the Remaining Staff

The key to the success of any MIS department is twofold. MIS must first understand the core business processes. Then MIS must understand the implications of changes in the political, social, and economical environments in relation to both the business processes and meeting customer needs. The people acting as liaisons between the outsourced vendor and the end users must acquire the business knowledge needed to effectively improve the service levels and to develop products that optimize the interactions between the end user and the customer.

Traditionally, MIS people view themselves as experts of technology and rarely recognize the need to understand the business, often perceiving this task as the end user's job. In today's business environment, the successful companies are those whose employees are customer-focused. MIS personnel cannot develop and deliver effective products to the end user without understanding the customer needs. The existing MIS personnel must be refocused to better serve the customer, through the end user.

MIS Personnel Must Have a Customer Focus.

A cultural change must occur in order to focus MIS personnel on the customer. The implication of this statement is well beyond the expertise of most MIS departments, yet it is the most significant challenge they face and the key to their success. This change requires the use of consultants specializing in organizational development and organizational change. These consultants can assist with the development of strategies and action plans that will effect a cultural change.

In addition, the existing personnel must be retooled in today's technologies (such as client/server, sysplexed systems, image processing, voice recognition) so they can leverage their ability to meet the needs of today's dynamic business environment. Understanding the new technologies and the user's business needs provides the basis for exploiting these technologies.

Hiring New Staff

The initial hiring must involve staffing of key management positions. The skills required for these positions have changed and differ significantly from the traditional MIS skills. These individuals must be both service-oriented and strategic thinkers who possess business acumen, leadership, and entrepreneurial skills. These individuals must have a proven track record of strong project management skills and a conceptual understanding of organizational development.

Organizational development provides the tools for enabling management to develop a strategy for structuring the organization, with emphasis on performance management, reward and compensation, processes and methodologies, metrics, and measurement.

Look for People With Strong Management *and* Strong Technical Skills: Never Settle for Less Than the Best.

While these qualities sound like a job for individuals with a master's in business administration (MBA), these are the skills required to transition the MIS department from a monopoly on technology to a business partner capable of leveraging technology to create business opportunities and meet new business challenges. This skill set serves as a complement to the technical skills.

People with strong technical skills must be acquired. Technology must be recognized as the means to deliver value-adding products to the end user. In today's environment, people with knowledge of client/server technology, data warehousing, and data mining are critical in support of the leadership role the MIS department must assume in the company. Tomorrow's environment might require different technical skills.

While the outsourcer looks like a good source of employees for the new MIS department, it will not provide many people. Very few of the outsourcer's staff will consider moving to the new MIS department. This is different from the start of the outsourcing effort. When the outsourcing took place, the existing MIS staff did not have a lot of time to evaluate the outsourcer as an employer. Additionally, since the MIS function was being outsourced, all of the MIS staff knew their days were numbered. Outsourcer personnel see an entirely different set of circumstances. First, they have been working with the client for quite some time so they already have formed an opinion of the client. This opinion will have been influenced by the client's dissatisfaction with the outsourcer's services, so, to be blunt, most outsourcer personnel will not think highly of the client and will not want to go to work for them. Second, unless the outsourcer is on shaky financial ground, the outsourcer employees will have no reason to think that their current position is at risk, so they will not be inclined to even look for another position.

Finding the right people in a timely fashion will be a difficult task. The new MIS department cannot count on filling all of the open positions in a timely fashion. Therefore, the MIS management should do extra planning to ensure that they perform effectively at any staffing level.

Bring the Processing Back Home

This is the reverse of the outsourcing activity. It will not be as smooth as the outsource. Although all of the equipment will be functioning, very few of the manual procedures will be in force.

There will also be a lack of documentation and an extreme lack of expertise. These factors substantially compound the difficulty of the insourcing effort.

When the outsource took place, the client had a trained staff running and maintaining the systems. This will not be the case during the insource. The client's staff will mostly be made up of new personnel unfamiliar with the systems and procedures. The outsourcer's staff will be available to assist, but they will be shorthanded—that is the nature of this beast—and many of them will not be very familiar with the systems.

This move should be undertaken very slowly and deliberately. Unfortunately, the client will be anxious to leave the outsourcer, because at this point the outsourcer is costing a lot of money. Remember, the client already has a new MIS staff and equipment, and is therefore paying about double for its processing capacity. Upper management will not want this to continue for very long. And everyone wants to get going on their own as fast as possible. Rushing at this point is to be expected, but it must be prevented.

Insourcing Requires Much More Planning Than Outsourcing.

The insourcing effort should be planned as meticulously as the outsourcing effort was. It should also take into consideration every problem and solution encountered during the outsourcing. Keep in mind that the majority of the MIS staff are new; that all of the manual procedures need to be written, modified, and tested; and that there will be missing utility software.

While it is possible to transfer everything over to the new MIS department in one quick move, it may not be desirable to do so. This is especially true if MIS is continuing to use established execution platforms and software. MIS should plan on a phased migration to the new order if it is at all possible. Consider the following hypothetical MIS environment.

The processing environment is MVS and the client uses CICS, TSO, and DB2. A conservative insource schedule might look like the following.

1. Connect new MVS machine to outsource data center using VTAM.
2. Insource application/maintenance programmers using VTAM gateway from in-house MVS to outsource MVS. This uses the client's MVS machine only as a gateway, while all files and programs reside on the outsourcer's MVS machine.
3. Create a CICS region on the client's MVS machine. Connect it to the outsourcer's MVS machine and run all of the client's users through a CICS terminal-owning region.
4. Move the CICS programs and databases over to the client's MVS machine. Now the users are actually executing their CICS transactions on the client's MVS machine.
5. Copy the remaining files and programs to the client's MVS machine.

Finer gradations are possible depending on how conservative the new MIS department wants to be. One benefit of the above approach is that there is no "Big Bang," so there is always plenty of time to resolve any issues that crop up. Another benefit is that the operations staff has time to adjust to the processing requirements. A third benefit is that the development staff incurs environmental changes over a long period of time, and this reduces their error rates. The problem with this approach is that the dual costs associated with insourcing and outsourcing are endured for a longer period of time. However, if the majority of the outsourcer costs are based on resource utilization, then the extra cost should not be very large.

6

Was Outsourcing a Good Idea?

In general, outsourcing was a good idea if the client made it through a complete contract and either considered or executed a second contract. But even if it was a good idea, it does not mean it was the best idea. The client may have considered or executed a second contract because insourcing would have been too expensive or required too many changes in the client's organizational structure.

The client may have terminated the outsourcing agreement even if everything was satisfactory. There are many reasons that this could happen. The client could have reorganized or entered a new market. Even a tax law change could spur the insource.

> ## A Single Change in Tax Laws Could Destroy the Financial Advantage to Outsource.

It is not always easy to tell whether the outsourcing experience was positive or negative until the numbers are analyzed. Once again it boils down to metrics. What about the financial aspects of outsourcing? Well, what better metric has been invented than the accounting of money? Finance has its own metrics, so let's start there.

Money isn't everything. Regardless of what the finance department thinks, a product cannot always be judged by its market value. Some things have an intrinsic worth that cannot easily be assigned a monetary value. So after looking at the money, the other metrics must be checked. (See Figure 6-1.)

Money Is Not Everything!

Analyzing the Costs

While projecting future costs is mostly smoke and mirrors (Figure 6-2), tracking actual costs is, or should be, straightforward. The complication resides in arguing the speculative alternative costs. Alternative costs include the anticipated employee burdens, the development capitalizations, and the depreciations. In other words, the difficulty associated with checking actual monies spent is the tax consequences of each decision. With this thought in mind, the starting point should be the total dollars spent. Once this amount is known, the monies can be categorized and the alternatives annotated.

Some companies are incapable of accounting for monies spent on their own MIS department. With an outsourcer, this is no longer a problem. The bottom-line cost of the outsourcer is the actual amount of monies paid out. It is imperative that the service level be left out of this calculation. In other words, no allowance should be made for goodwill.

To calculate whether the outsourcing experience was a success, match the monies spent each month or quarter against the amounts projected at the contract start. Scale each of these values by their current NPV. Compare the resulting amount to the

Figure 6-1. Projected outsourcing savings.

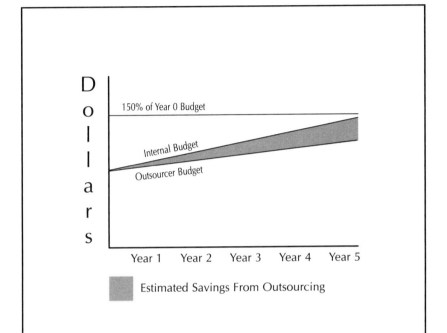

When the outsourcing effort is being investigated, a chart some-what like this one will be generated. The costs will approximate linear increases as time goes on, and the slope of the outsourcer's cost will be less than the MIS function.

The projected savings are represented by the shaded area and are getting bigger and bigger as time goes on. The natural conclusion from this diagram is that the savings from outsourcing will acceler-ate as time goes on.

This type of projection is extremely hard to refute. But because it is so positive in nature, it leads to large-scale disappointment if the projections are not realized.

Figure 6-2. Probable spending pattern.

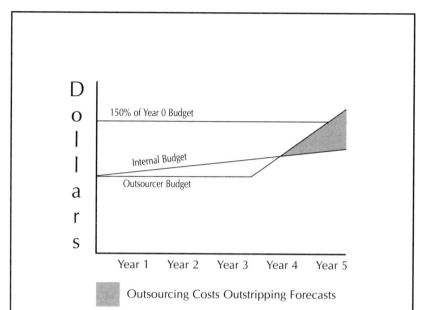

This diagram projects the most probable cost profile. The outsourcer cost remains fairly close to the projected growth curve in the early stages of the contract. However, around the midpoint of the contract, several factors start to accelerate the cost of the outsourcing agreement.

It has been shown many times in the past that 80 percent of all projects in MIS fail in one or more of their deliverables. Outsourcing is just another form of project, so it will also fail 80 percent of the time. What makes MIS spectacular in its failures is the speed with which it moves from being on time and within budget to absolute disaster. It will be the same with outsourcing.

The causes of this have been covered earlier, but the major causes should be stated again: inadequate requirements, slowly falling service levels, and failing communications.

estimated or actual amount stated in the outsourcing contract. If the NPV of the actual amounts is higher than the NPV amount referenced in the outsourcing contract, the outsourcing effort was not a success.

The costs specified in the original outsource contract must be more than what was actually spent, not just equal to it. The amount projected in the original contract was probably based on best-case scenarios. Human nature, and company politics in particular, require that all amounts presented to or by upper management be guaranteed results. This strategy highlights differences so that decisions can be made without undue agonizing over the correctness of terms. Or, using the current vernacular, people like decisions to be *slam dunks.*

The Outsourcer Must Meet or Beat the Contract Amounts.

The reality of the situation is as follows. When a guaranteed result claim is made, it is made with the understanding that nothing could ever go wrong and that the other alternatives can not even come close. When playing by these rules it is necessary to be totally unforgiving or MIS will find itself outsourced once again—thus the hard-nosed attitude. If the outsourcer could not beat the numbers they published in the contract, numbers that everyone would have agreed would be impossible not to beat, then outsourcing must truly have been a bad decision from a financial standpoint.

Is it possible to have a successful financial side to outsourcing? Yes, depending on the competence of the prior MIS staff. If the former staff was completely out of control, then outsourcing can be financially successful. Otherwise, the answer is probably no. Is this a harsh view? Yes it is, but it is probably a realistic view.

Checking the Service Level

If adequate metrics had been adopted for tracking the service level, this section would not be necessary. If adequate metrics were in place, chances are pretty good that the outsourcing relationship would still be ongoing. Therefore, we can assume two things. The first is that the service level deteriorated. The second is that the level dropped to one that was unacceptably low, but that the circumstances that brought the service level down were (or are) unmeasurable.

Now is the time to review all of the problems encountered during the outsourcing. If the low service level was not prevented, it can at least be taken through a post mortem so that something can be learned from it. All problem reports generated throughout the life of the outsource should be reviewed. These reports should be categorized by type and then analyzed for priority, time to fix, cost to fix, type of fix, and result of fix. These problems were the main cause of the insource, but they do not go away just because the client is insourcing. Some of them do go away—those that were related to the interface between two companies. However, keep in mind that the primary reason for the original outsource was probably because MIS was out of control. It is ridiculous to allow this to happen again, especially after such a large, expensive, and extended-duration lesson (the outsourcing) was paid for.

The Service Level Must Continuously Increase.

By reviewing these problem reports, the client can create a new set of service level metrics which, if kept up to date, can assist MIS in staying insourced and keep the user community happy.

Two other areas need consideration: user satisfaction and application development. These areas both reflect and influence the service level, so it is necessary to consider each independently.

User Satisfaction

User dissatisfaction, combined with company politics, was the driving force behind the initial outsourcing arrangement. Looking at the service level and determining the decline is a formal technique for determining if the outsourcer is living up to the contract terms. However, checking up on user satisfaction is probably more important. User satisfaction is never guaranteed. In fact, MIS can assume that the user is never satisfied. However, there are levels of dissatisfaction. If the level of user satisfaction is adjusted for the fact that no user is ever satisfied, it can become a very valid metric. Unfortunately, this is very seldom done and as such means that most outsourcers (and client management) perceive the user as being dissatisfied.

> ## Users Are Never Satisfied But They Must Be Less Dissatisfied.

The question pertaining to the outsourcing agreement is not whether the user was satisfied, but if the user was more or less satisfied than before the outsourcing took place. If the user was as satisfied as before, the outsourcer was doing fine. If the user was more satisfied than before, the outsourcer is doing great. If the user was less satisfied than before, the outsourcer is in big trouble (remembering that the client outsourced because of user dissatisfaction).

> # Upper Management May Not Care About User Satisfaction.

If the user ended up being less satisfied with the outsourcer than with MIS, the outsourcing was not a good idea. After all, one of the primary reasons for outsourcing was to make the user happier. On the other hand, if the user was less satisfied with the outsourcer, management has decided that there are other things more important than user satisfaction.

Application Development

Application development has a solid history of late delivery, excess costs, and inadequate features. An analysis of the development that took place under the outsourcer needs to be viewed in this light. Specifically, this is one area where the outsourcer probably fares no worse than if the development groups had not been outsourced. In fact, one should expect either a maintenance of the status quo or an actual improvement (in every aspect except the monies). If the outsourcer is very strong in development, the client will come out ahead. Remember that the single largest reason for development overruns is inadequate requirements identification and that two thirds of the cause for this rests on the user side. Outsourcers that have a strong background in development understand this situation and take steps, in a rather normal and pedantic fashion, to ensure that this does not affect their projects.

> # The Outsourcer Must Always Understand All the User Requirements.

Outsourcers that protect themselves against the client's users will provide better application development results than the client was able to furnish. Outsourcers that do not understand this will have worse application development results than the client. Simple metrics tracking work effort, defects, and schedule slippage should easily show these results. In fact, if the outsourcer is going to be more successful than the client in development, it will probably be much more successful.

If it is not much more successful, the outsourcing of application development was not successful. Having an outsourcer deliver systems that cost more, are late, and are sub-functional signals a total failure. After all, the internal MIS staff could have delivered these same results and still have had a better working relationship with the end users.

Checking the Company Welfare

Of the topics covered in this section, company welfare is the most important. Did the outsourcing help or hurt the company? Looking at the money does not tell the whole story. Outsourcing could have saved the company money but hurt the company at the same time. The same principle applies to service level: A high service level does not mean the company's welfare improved.

Outsourcing has a tendency to reduce the flexibility of a company to respond to MIS-related circumstances. Did this inflexibility help or hurt the company welfare? If the client's MIS function was stressing the company structure and finances and the outsourcing put a stop to this, then outsourcing was probably good for the company welfare. If the company's product is intimately related to the MIS services and the business is highly competitive, then outsourcing probably hurt the company's welfare.

Of course, these items are much more complicated than those two previous examples. But the general rule could be:

❖ Companies whose MIS functions are geared towards the back office or simply supporting the business can benefit from good outsourcing environments.

❖ Companies whose business product depends on the use of MIS functions cannot benefit from the outsourcing environment.

Rigid Outsourcers Hurt the Client.

In many circumstances these two rules do not apply, and most MIS managers can easily determine when they apply to their organizations.

The main point of this discussion is that outsourcing is not always a question of money or service level but of what is appropriate. Outsourcing may be a good deal financially but a bad deal for the company. Outsourcing may improve the service level but may restrict the flexibility needed to support the company.

When considering outsourcing, a company should look at the money, the service level, the need for flexibility, and the personnel. Why the personnel? Presumably they are the people who caused the company to consider outsourcing. It might just be cheaper and better all around to invest the outsourcing effort and money back into the existing MIS function.

However, such a venture cannot be taken lightly. The company must understand the ramifications of making such an investment. Rebuilding MIS is more complicated than building an organization from scratch. Rebuilding requires a culture change, and a culture change requires management commitment and fortitude to see the effort through to completion.

7

Protecting
Against
Insourcing

The biggest causes of insourcing are a declining service level and a lack of flexibility on the part of the outsourcer in achieving the goals of the client. Of course, the latter is also perceived as a declining service level. Protecting against insourcing reduces to maintaining the service level. If the service level is adequate, there is little justification for insourcing.

It turns out that protecting the service level is entirely within the client's domain, but it must be recognized as such during the initial contract negotiation. Recognizing this fact later predisposes the client to being critical of the service level. If the protection of the service level is not explicitly recognized in the contract, the client has no mechanism for controlling the quality of the outsource effort. If the quality cannot be controlled, the client should simply insource the work and terminate the outsourcing agreement.

There are two major points that must be made about protecting the service level. The first is that the outsourcer must be paid enough to be able to provide the expected service level. The second is that the outsourcer must be compelled to plan for providing the expected service level. The two points are completely interrelated.

Business Relationships

Business relationships can work in one of two ways. The first is that a company can attempt to get the absolute best deal it can from a supplier, regardless of whether that deal puts the supplier at risk. This relationship is good when the product being supplied is a commodity and can be supplied by anyone. The second relationship is one where the product is only available from a few suppliers, so the client needs to ensure the well-being of the supplier. In this circumstance, if the supplier fails, the client suffers.

Outsourcing relationships are of the second kind. Any financial arrangement that jeopardizes the outsourcer affects the client. The outsourcer cannot be considered a commodity; it must be treated as an integral part of the client's business. In other words, the outsourcer must be considered to be a partner of the client. While there has been a lot of hype in the media about outsourcers becoming partners of their clients, in reality this actually happens very infrequently. Maintaining a partnership requires a lot of work on the part of a client. The client cannot sign the contract and expect it to be executed worry-free. The client must be an active participant in the agreement. This runs counter to the notion that a company can outsource MIS and live happily ever after.

Outsourcers Must Be Paid Enough to Improve Their Business.

We can see how successful outsourcing agreements work in other industries by looking at the relationship between manufacturers and their parts suppliers. During the late 1970s, American automobile manufacturers determined that they needed to improve the quality of their products. One of the first actions they took was to mandate to their suppliers that the quality of incoming parts had to improve. However, many of these manufacturers were using the suppliers with the lowest available costs, and these suppliers were not making enough profit on their sales to afford to make the necessary improvements. Secondly, these suppliers were not sure exactly what the manufacturers really meant by quality. After all, quality is often in the eye of the beholder. What finally happened is that manufacturers started working with suppliers on a continuing basis to define quality and to ensure it *and* the manufacturers agreed to *pay* for the increased quality. The end product of this partnering effort was actually two improvements. First, the quality of the parts did improve. Second, the cost of the added quality was soon less than the price of the original parts simply because the quality was so high.

Contractual Terms

The contract provides the framework on which the partnership is built. The foundation of this framework is the terms. Terms consist of the amounts of monies and the amount and types of services. While most people concentrate on whole dollar amounts, these are really a reflection of the amount and types of services being performed. Amounts and types of services are what defines the service level. The client should be most concerned with the service levels, then the monies. The monies must be considered only after the service levels are defined; if this is not the case, then the monies will define the service levels. This places the client in the situation where it has already agreed in principle to a lower level of service than it needs. Thus, the service-level definitions must come first; only with their complete specification can the client decide that it can afford to outsource. While each client is different, there are some general service-level requirements to which every outsourcer should be held.

The client must take several steps to protect both itself and the outsourcer. The first step is procedural. The client must specify that the outsourcer perform certain functions and provide certain basic services, and these must be measurable and reportable to the client. The second step is that the client must maintain an organization that monitors the outsourcer closely enough to certify that the terms of the contract are being maintained. Finally, and just as important, the client must be willing to pay for these functions and services. It makes no sense to require services that the outsourcer cannot afford to provide.

> # Outsourcers Must Have Excess Processing Capacity, Guaranteed Priorities, Adequate Staffing, and Thorough Development Tools.

The client must require that the outsourcer provide the following:

1. Maintain an excess processing capacity at a given level. This level is dependent on the type of load the client's processing places on the outsourcer's machines. For instance, if the client's processing is mostly batch, then the outsourcer might need to maintain only an additional 10 or 20 percent capacity on its machines. But if the client's main processing requirements are on-line systems, then the outsourcer might need to maintain an additional 50 percent capacity to ensure adequate response times under all conditions.

2. Maintain a priority structure that guarantees the client access to the resources and personnel needed to support its work. Resources consist of CPU, I/O, communications, and distribution. Personnel consist of technical support staff, development staff, and *experts*. While an efficient outsourcer will utilize its personnel and resources across all of its clients, this technique

will always penalize the average client. The penalty is related to the fact that every request for additional personnel and resources will require that the other clients give up some of the service that they are receiving. And since each client is usually *one of the other clients,* this means they will be penalized on a regular basis. Thus it is imperative that the client require either top priority on all of its needs or that the outsourcer provide dedicated, non-generic resources and personnel.

3. Certification of adequate staffing and machine capacity before any additional clients are solicited and again before they enter into another client/outsourcer relationship. This could be as extreme as being given access to new contracts to ensure that the client's rights have not been superseded. Each new client increases the work load on the outsourcer's equipment, personnel, and management. While economies of scale allow the outsourcer to improve its profits by adding clients, it means that with each added client, each existing client is losing access to resources and personnel. It also means that the existing clients have just been bumped down in priority in the eyes of the outsourcer. The right of the client to engage in a certification of the outsourcer is certainly intrusive and will be resisted by the outsourcer. Therefore, this certification must be made as palatable as possible, even though it is an extremely serious requirement.

Consider the following: The client has two relationships with the outsourcer. The first is the service-level relationship, where the outsourcer agrees to provide X amount of service in Y timely fashion. The second is the more intimate relationship, the partnership between the two parties. This partnership is somewhat like a marriage or a romance. When the outsourcer adds another client it is adding another partner. It is not possible for this new partner to exist outside of the current relationship between the client and outsourcer.

Certification is an absolute necessity. Without certification the client has no protection from the outsourcer's natural expansionist tendency. Each expansion entails risk along with opportunity. It is imperative that the outsourcer not endanger its own health without consulting its clients. Otherwise, each client can find itself out of business without any prior indication of risk. Lest one think that this is a needless worry, one only need to look at the age of the current outsourcers; most are very young, but outsourcing under one name or another has been around for thirty years.

4. Implement development tools for ensuring the ongoing success of any systems or applications development activities. At a minimum, these development tools should consist of a set of formal processes and a set of software metrics designed to monitor and report the development status. It is a sad but true fact that most development projects come in late and over budget. It is also true that the users of these systems are almost always taken by surprise by the magnitude of these overruns.

Users Are Always Surprised By the Magnitude of the Overruns.

When an overrun occurs within a company, it is often made more palatable because the users can affect the budgets of the MIS groups involved. The users have some recourse, and because MIS is from their own company they are willing to forgive and forget, at least to some extent. When an overrun occurs with the outsourcer, the only thing the client sees is an increased cost. Furthermore, since there are fewer communications channels between the client's users and the outsourcer than when MIS was developing the systems, users have even less idea of the status of the remaining activities for the development of the systems. This lack of communications combined with the hard costs of overruns mandate that the client and outsourcer have formal and complete procedures for performing development and reporting status.

The first three items in the above list are designed to protect the client from the well-meaning (but nonetheless impacting) effect of the outsourcer's natural expansion. It is okay for the outsourcer to expand, but the outsourcer must realize that it is now an integral part of the client's business. It is extremely common for the service level of an existing client to decline with each new client the outsourcer takes on.

Development Efforts Must Follow a Methodology.

The fourth item will force the outsourcer to reevaluate the way it conducts its own business. Formal, industry-standard development processes have been around for twenty years. Unfortunately, most companies either do not use them or use them incorrectly. In fact, most companies do not know how to use them correctly, so the problem is even bigger than it looks on the surface. Software metrics, which are used to provide feedback to improve the development processes, are not new, but are seldom used to measure development progress and almost never used to improve the development process. Even so, the use of software metrics does provide a clear look at the instantaneous status of a project, and their use should be considered a minimum requirement of the outsourcer.

Managing the Outsourcer

To provide complete protection against insourcing requires that the client actually get involved in the outsourcer's management activities. Ideally the outsourcer would adopt a policy of optimizing its quality- and service-level capacity. This would require a buy-in by the outsourcer's management and a tight relationship with its clients. There are three methods available for ac-

complishing this. The first is a formal technique generally referred to as ISO 9000. ISO 9000 is a standard quality guideline
that attempts to force an organization to formalize its quality
management methods. The second is the Capability Maturity
Model, which is a formalized methodology for identifying the
maturity of an MIS organization. The third is a new technique
based on the identification of those factors that determine an organization's ability to deliver service. The three methods complement one another and are described below.

ISO 9000

ISO 9000 is a standard designed to manage, audit, and certify
quality. ISO 9000 has three components. The first component
consists of adopting a quality management plan for the company or organization. The second component consists of creating
a management structure to implement the quality plan. The
third component consists of documenting that the quality plan is
being followed on a day-to-day basis. To put it all together, what
we get is that ISO 9000 consists of telling people how to perform
quality management, having them doing quality management,
and being able to prove that they are doing quality management.
The basic assumption is that if a company adopts ISO 9000, it
will be getting quality as a direct effect of executing the ISO 9000
process.

> ## ISO 9000 Does Not Guarantee Im-
> ## provements in Quality.

Every client should seek to find an ISO 9000–certified outsourcer. They should do so for several reasons. First, part of the
ISO 9000 certification requires annual audits to ensure that the
quality processes are continuing in force. Second, an outsourcer

that is ISO 9000-certified has at a minimum published how it is going to maintain quality and has agreed to maintain that quality. This public statement of quality and commitment is both aesthetically pleasing and contractually binding. If the outsourcer is ISO 9000–certified, the client will have both the knowledge of any impending problems (through the recertification process) and the right to demand compliance.

One small problem with ISO 9000 certification that is often not understood is that ISO 9000 certification does not guarantee quality; it only guarantees that a quality management program is in place. The difference is subtle but important. ISO 9000 certification does not mean that quality will improve. It only means that if quality deteriorates, it will be visible.

Capability Maturity Model

The Software Engineer's Institute (SEI) Capability Maturity Model (CMM) is utilized to determine the level of development maturity of an MIS organization. The underlying assumption of this methodology is that an organization can improve its development performance by modelling its procedures and methodologies after those described in CMM. The model assesses the maturity level based on the capability of the organization to achieve expected results by following a software process. The model also focuses on the performance of an organization in relation to the actual results. CMM assumes management processes are in place to support software process improvement and that people are capable, that is, skilled to support software process improvement.

The model defines five levels of maturity, each building on the other to maximize software process improvement. The initial level is characterized as ad hoc and chaotic and is personality dependent. Level two is crucial for establishing the infrastructure of software improvement and focuses on repeatability by implementing policies and procedures in support of a basic project management methodology. This level is characterized as disciplined. Level three is characterized as defined with standards documented and institutionalized in the organization. A level four organization is managed and measured, and the quality of the products is predictable. Level five organizations are characterized as being in a state of continuous process improvement. Some examples of level five organizations are those working on the space shuttle and air-to-ground missile projects. These organizations implement products with zero defects. They are also dealing with life-and-death situations.

> CMM Enables Organizations to Become Process Driven, Not Personality Driven.

As with ISO 9000, the SEI Capability Maturity Model is not a "how to" model but rather a means of keeping a scorecard on whether the guidelines of software development are followed. The model does not ensure software process improvement. However, for organizations that are personality dependent, this is an excellent means of institutionalizing processes and standards and improving productivity.

Service Level Capacity Index

The Service Level Capacity Index is a simple formula that describes an organization's current ability to provide service to a user. In this case, the organization would be the outsourcer and the user would be the client. The formula consists of the expertise of an organization divided by its complexity. The idea behind this is simple. If the complexity of an organization increases without a corresponding increase in expertise, the organization's ability to deliver service goes down. If this happens, the client will see a decline in service. On the other hand, if the expertise of an outsourcer goes up or the complexity of an outsourcer goes down, it will be able to provide more service to the client. The value of the index is somewhat subtle. On the surface it looks like the index provides only a reflection of the underlying factors. The importance is that the underlying factors are identified by the index, so it is possible for the outsourcer to actually make changes targeted to improve its service-level capacity.

The factors that make up the expertise of the outsourcer include the quality of the staff, the structure of the organization, the quality of the documentation, and the sophistication of the operating environment. Staff quality is based on two factors: knowledge of the business of the client and knowledge of data processing. These two factors are typically modelled by the number of years of each person in the two areas. The structure of the organization determines how smoothly information flows between personnel. Some organizational structures are good for communications, some are good for control, some are good for both, and some are good for nothing (unfortunately). Documentation assists the organization in disseminating information and knowledge. Appropriate and up-to-date documentation allows an organization to survive in a world of staff turnover. Good documentation backed up by the right organizational structure allows any organization to exist without the aid of personnel superstars. Sophistication of the operating environment makes a difference in the amount of service that a machine configuration can provide. This is a simple area to judge, but important nonetheless. If the operating environment is designed to facilitate a specific kind of work, then that type of work is easy to perform. Otherwise, the work is more difficult to perform.

The Service Level Capacity Index Is a Proactive Metric.

The factors that make up the complexity of the outsourcer are related to its internal procedures and its client work load.

These factors are related to the number and type of systems that need to be maintained. They consist of the number of systems, the size of each system (in terms of jobs, transactions, databases, tables); the interrelationships of those systems, both inter and intra; the number of unique environments (such as home-grown development tools, application support systems, and database systems); and the budget available to support these items. While the relationships between these factors is not linear, the concepts are. Increased counts of systems, sizes, interrelationships, unique environments, and budgets can only mean that it is harder to understand and change any single aspect. Obviously, if it is hard to change one thing, it is harder to change two, and so on. A complex environment requires more expertise, so complexity is something that should be decreased.

The value of the Service Level Capacity Index is that the factors on which it is based are identified. This means that the outsourcer can look at a given area, make a change on paper representing the expected results of a change, and see how its service level capacity is affected. For the first time ever an organization (in this case the outsourcer) can actually make a change without resorting to tea leaves to forecast the final effect.

Helping the Outsourcer Succeed

The entire focus of the client should be the success of the outsourcer. As long as the outsourcer is succeeding in providing the service level that the client needs, the client is succeeding. If the outsourcer fails, the client fails. It is obvious that the outsourcer and the client must be partners, and that the client must be an active partner, not passive. This means that the client cannot execute the contract and then sit back and wait for it to succeed. Many companies realize this and use simple service-level metrics to provide a contractual definition of performance by the outsourcer. The problem with this approach is that it is a passive measurement of service. A metric approach simply provides a reflection of the current situation—it does not provide any mechanism to correct a deteriorating situation.

Clients need to realize that in addition to monitoring the performance of the outsourcer, they must be in a position to actively improve the outsourcer's service level. Outsourcing contracts must provide for both management and technical solutions in addition to simple monetary penalties when service drops. Contracts should also provide for expanded service at reduced cost. Clients also need to understand that they probably misled the outsourcer about the amount of work to be performed in the first place.

> ## If the Outsourcer Fails, the Client Has Failed.

The client and the outsourcer are partners. Partners need full communication and shared responsibility. Full communication requires that tools like ISO 9000, CMM, and the Service Level Capacity Index be utilized by the outsourcer. Shared responsibility requires that the client take an active part in the management of its needs with the outsourcer. The idea that a client can turn over the work and simply write out a check has to be firmly renounced. While most clients say they understand this point, their actions indicate that they do not. These clients are bound to fail in their outsourcing efforts. Clients that actually do understand this point are those that have the best chance of succeeding in their outsourcing.

> ## Some Clients Don't Care if the Outsourcer Succeeds.

8

Protecting Against Outsourcing

Decisions to outsource are oftentimes highly political; in fact, they are almost totally political. MIS rarely has representation at the executive level. Traditionally, MIS departments are aligned under the Chief Financial Officer (CFO); thus, all of their policies, successes, and failures are represented to the executive team via a proxy. Typically, the proxy representing MIS does not have a data processing background, so he is incapable of adequately representing or defending the actions of MIS. In turn, MIS does not possess enough financial savvy to demonstrate its contribution to the profit margin in financial terms. Therefore, very few executives credit MIS with earning money for the company. This "Catch-22" scenario of the proxy not having data processing knowledge and MIS not demonstrating value added in financial terms creates a perception that MIS is an overhead cost instead of an income generator.

Another contributing factor results from the technical skill requirements of MIS. MIS staff are highly paid compared with other departments in the company. These factors, coupled with budget overruns and late delivery of products, send up flares that highlight MIS as an area to be closely scrutinized for trimming expenses.

Against this backdrop of ignorance and bias it is difficult for MIS to protect itself from being outsourced. Under these circumstances, MIS must come to the realization that *MIS has no say in whether or not it will be outsourced.*

MIS must understand what the contributing factors are for deciding to outsource and the role it has played in contributing to the decision if it wishes to prevent itself from being outsourced.

The following actions should place MIS on a better footing with the other departments within a company. Once this *more equal* status is achieved, MIS will have a better chance of charting its own destiny.

Back to Basics—The Three Ms

Management, methodology, and metrics are the starting points for establishing credibility with executive management. While these concepts are not innovative, they are guaranteed to help meet the objectives of the MIS department. Methodology and metrics are the tools effective management employ to meet client needs.

Management

Management in this context is associated with the people who manage. People who manage have many styles and vary in the degree of their effectiveness. Management also includes several universal properties. Even though management comprises these properties, styles, and processes, it always involves working with people. While the people aspects of management are not covered in depth in this book, they are still an integral part of management. The table on the next page provides a high-level description of the core competencies required for effectively managing work, people, and leadership.

Each of the skills identified in the above table require discipline and commitment to the associated methodologies. Managers must recognize what motivates an individual. They must identify the strengths and weaknesses of the individuals and must recognize the opportunity for improving the level of their confidence and further developing the individuals' understanding of their contribution to the organization. In setting expectations, managers must set clearly defined goals with measurable and quantifiable

Management Core Competencies

Managing Work	Managing Employees	Leadership
Business case development	Performance management	Business acumen
Project management	Employee development	Conflict management
Accountability	Performance assessment	Negotiation skills
Innovation	Performance compensation	Strategic thinking
Supplier management	Goal setting	Entrepreneurial skills
System integration	Clearly defined expectations	Communication skills Interpersonal skills

objectives. Managers must follow through in monitoring progress and coach and mentor when the progress is not made or reward when expectations are exceeded. Most importantly, managers must hold individuals accountable for the level of work performed. The performance review must accurately reflect whether the goals and objectives were met or whether they were exceeded. If the expectations were not met, then appropriate action must be taken to correct the failures, either through disciplinary action or reduction in salary and position. If the expectations were exceeded then there should be adequate compensation and rewards.

Most managers fail to follow the methodologies for managing people; they are time-consuming and require a dedication to the success of others. If managers can step up to the task of properly managing people they will gain increases in productivity and a commitment from their people to achieve goals and objectives.

Management must keep abreast of trends in the MIS business in order to take advantage of opportunities as they present themselves. While making a case to protect against outsourcing, good management includes an awareness of all the alternatives that reduce costs and speed up delivery. Dependent on the scope of effort, outsourcing is a viable alternative to reduce the costs associated with non-value-added work, including tasks such as code construction and unit and string testing, given that MIS has completely defined the result it needs. These tasks might be performed offshore where the cost of labor is significantly cheaper. In turn this allows key individuals to be utilized in the core work of providing business solutions through technology.

Methodologies

Methodologies are templates for planning. They provide a road map to success and are a set of ordered activities. Adopting a methodology, virtually any methodology, is imperative. The methodology must include efforts in which the user areas must participate. The methodology walks MIS and the users through a series of activities where requirements can be viewed. The benefits derived from this process are many: The users recognize their role in the development cycle, and MIS gains business knowledge, guarantees items are not overlooked, and, foremost, ensures that very few new requirements enter the development effort later in the project (when they would cost much more to address).

Any methodology will get the job done. However, the effectiveness of the methodology lies in the discipline of MIS to adhere to the methodology. Two methodologies are discussed below: a software development methodology and project management methodology.

Methodologies Provide Road Maps to Success.

The following table identifies a software development methodology that addresses both a traditional life cycle approach coupled with a parallel quality assurance approach beginning during the development phase. While these approaches are separate efforts with specific tasks, their overall effectiveness lies in the ability of the approaches to interact in such a manner that information is exchanged. The overall benefits include reducing costs by identifying errors early in the development during the reviews, where it is cheaper to correct, and by ensuring that the test cases provide an adequate level of complexity to minimize errors in production.

Software Development Methodology

Development Life Cycle	*Test Life Cycle*
Business Case & Analysis	Test Planning
Prioritization & Planning	Review & Approval
Infrastructure	Requirements
Select Architecture, Products, Tools	Design
Products	Test Plan
Tools	Test Environment
Configuration	Environment Preparation
Acquire Products	Environment Set Up
Development	Execution & Verification
Requirements	Functional Test
Analysis	User Acceptance
Design	Performance Test
Product Selection	System Test
Acquire Product	Test Metrics
Construction	Defect Tracking
Unit Testing	Risk Assessment
String/Integration Testing	Implementation Support
Implementation	Deployment Support
Deployment	

While documentation is not mentioned in each phase, it is imperative that documentation occurs throughout the methodology and that it is accurate, clearly stated, and maintainable.

Each of these phases must be documented to maximize throughput during the subsequent phases and to minimize the learning curve as new people are added to the development and maintenance efforts.

Enable People to Be Portable. Put the Knowledge Into the Documentation.

A separate life cycle for testing requires dedicated people whose primary focus is ensuring that the client's requirements are met. The test life cycle begins when the high-level design has been completed, with a formal turnover to the test group, which includes all documentation. Subsequent phases of the development life cycle involve the test group. The test group becomes part of the approval process for subsequent documentation. A test plan is developed, and the test environment is prepared during the construction phase of the software. A concurrent test life cycle will reduce the overall development cycle time and increase the probability of delivering the product on time.

The project management methodology focuses on the fundamental premise of planning and managing the associated activities to ensure that a project meets user requirements and that the requirements are developed in a timely and efficient manner. Considering how long this has been known, it is surprising how often it does not get done. Somewhere along the years of development, MIS lost sight of these basic premises. MIS became overconfident in its ability to identify the scope of the work, estimate the time to complete a project, and know the number of resources required. MIS relies on the same people, does not leverage the knowledge, and thinks that documentation is not needed because the people are already familiar with the required functionality. MIS also thinks that people come through in a crisis and, more importantly, that they know all the nuances and idiosyncrasies of the system. Compounding the effect of this misguided reliance, which is based on a can-do attitude and a strong degree of overconfidence, is the simple fact that everything in data processing has been continually increasing in complexity. It is a small wonder that MIS lacks credibility when championing new activities and a smaller wonder still that so many projects are not achieved on time, within budget, and with the required functionality. It is imperative that MIS management regain sight of these basic premises.

Planning

Project management *planning* defines the work, the roles and responsibilities, and the milestones and deliverables. This allows for readily identifying when and where a breakdown in the plan has occurred and provides the insight necessary for effectively making corrections.

The plan must be flexible with regard to project scope, cost, and time, and incorporate contingencies for change control. Three primary factors can change the plan: a change in the scope of effort, a change in the available resources, or a change in technology. Scope creep (the slow addition of requirements) is directly correlated with insufficient involvement by the users during the development of the business case. The effects of requirement changes must be demonstrated in dollars and project schedules. The users must be involved in the prioritization process to fully recognize the implications of their requests. The longer the project takes, the more flexible the plan must be. If projects generally take too long, MIS might consider using techniques that are known to reduce the approval and development time. One such technique, prototyping, when utilized as a proof of concept, can speed up the approval process and lock in client requirements in a fairly short time frame. A change in technology, for instance, a shift from mainframe to client/server, can significantly affect the project plan, as this affects the definition of work, roles and responsibilities, the milestones, and deliverables. Other technological changes, such as a new tool, may influence the project schedule regarding the time to deliver.

However, allowing for such contingencies in the initial planning will reduce delays in delivery of the product.

> ## Scope Creep Is the Single Biggest Cause of Failed Projects.

Metrics

Metrics are the vehicle MIS management uses to demonstrate the value provided by MIS functions. Metrics provide an objective and unbiased view of where the money is spent and what benefits are associated with the MIS effort. Metrics also allow the client organization to readily see the impacts of changes in requirements and the addition of new projects to the current work load. On the MIS side, metrics enable MIS to more accurately estimate the time and cost relative to requested changes and new work.

Software development usually occurs in an environment that does not have checks and balances, internally or externally, for measuring success. Software development in the majority of companies is a function that supports the core business processes. Rarely is software development conducted in a strict and controlled environment, and even less likely is the probability that the development effort is run *like a business.* If the development effort is run like a business, with profit and loss statements, outsourcing becomes unnecessary.

> ## Metrics Provide a Mechanism for Supporting Development Quality and Costing Charge-Back.

The only way to develop metrics is to start logging time against efforts. As previously mentioned in Chapter 3, at a minimum even a best guess at what each phase in the development and test life cycles cost on the last project will serve as a baseline. Actually, the project just completed is the best starting point, as management is probably thinking about all the things it could have done to make it better.

While it is important to establish a baseline, it is more important to develop the discipline needed by the MIS staff to track their own time against efforts. Depending on the culture of the MIS department, time tracking may need to be incorporated into the performance plan as a measurable proficiency until it becomes second nature to track time against effort. Developing timesheets and making them mandatory is an alternative for tracking costs.

However drastic the measures may be perceived to get the information, recognize that without this crucial information MIS will never gain control of its destiny.

Convert to a Value Center
and Activity-Based Costing

MIS must change its position from being a cost center to being a value center. A value center focuses on operations, productivity, and sound financial investments. The primary financial goal of the value center is to contribute to the Return On Equity, or ROE. The ROE drives the stock price, which is the ultimate measure of success. While MIS cannot control financial investments, it can contribute to controlling costs associated with operation and productivity. MIS must determine whether the work it is doing adds value. MIS must be able to reconcile the cost of doing the work versus the benefits gained and must answer two fundamental questions: What will be the return on the investment in a project and how is a project ranked or deemed as adding value, therefore warranting the investment?

Two financial tools, Net Present Value, or NPV, and Internal Rate of Return, IRR, can be utilized for identifying value-adding work. Both of these tools address the concept of "time value of money." The time value of money concept assesses the value of investing in one venture over another based on interest and rate of return for each investment. This concept answers the question, "If I invest today, what is the worth of that investment over time?" The greater the return over the period of time for which the investment is made, the greater the value the investment offers. The IRR is a means of rating projects internal to the company. While MIS will not be going to an external lender for funds, the corporation, in essence, will be funding the project and must earn a return on the investment. The internal rate of return is equal to the risk the corporation will take in fronting the money for a project. The risk includes the basic risk associated with Treasury bills, a minimum of 3 to 4 percent, plus some additional percentage points for the level of risk.

Fundamentally this comes back to identifying the costs of doing business. An understanding of basic financial models and concepts provides a means of self-evaluation by MIS. The financial concept of *activity-based costing* is identifying the direct and indirect costs associated with work. All costs must be identified, including the costs incurred by the client organizations. Once again this provides the opportunity for the client to share in the responsibility of defining the value the work will add to the company. Cost/benefit analysis is part of the business case process. The client must develop the business case to justify the work being requested. MIS is available to provide information regarding the assets and resources needed for the work defined in the business case; however, the client must provide the justification. The business case must also identify the productivity improvements or savings, either as hard-earned savings or savings in avoided costs.

> ## MIS Must Charge for Their Services and the Charges Must Go Against the Specific Users.

MIS must be capable of accurately representing the costs of MIS resources, accurately estimating the cost for developing products, and ensuring a timely delivery (Figure 8-1). Timely delivery is crucial to the client organization since the organization will forecast savings based on a reduction in staffing or efficiencies that may be introduced through new systems functionality.

A formal change control process coupled with a chargeback system between the client organization and MIS provides a method to monitor and track responsibilities of each partner. Change control enforces the accountability of each partner, enables the service level measurements, and assesses the impact of changes in requirements. In turn, chargebacks to MIS for Client Minutes of Interruption (CMI), resulting from software or hardware failures, will create a focus on quality assurance with regard to software development and hardware upgrades.

Focusing on transitioning to a value center demonstrates that MIS is in control of its costs and has the tools to reduce costs and make process improvements. This also demonstrates that MIS has the discipline to manage activities that contribute to the company's return on equity.

Market MIS to Upper Management

Upper management perceives MIS as a high-cost, low-service, low-quality organization. It continually takes the position that it does not understand what MIS does, and that while it needs computers, MIS is too expensive and usually needs to be controlled. MIS is perceived as too expensive. This is why so many MIS organizations are directly under the control of the finance department. While it is true that MIS runs the General Ledger and AP and AR systems, it is also true that MIS runs the manufacturing systems, the customer service systems, the personnel systems, and the systems upon which the company's day-to-day livelihood depends. In other words, upper management seeks only to control the MIS costs while relegating the benefits that

Figure 8-1. Dollar cost of late development.

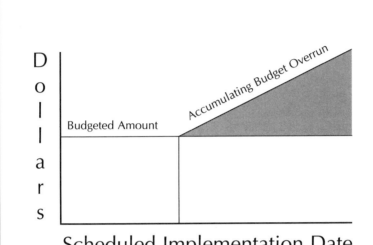

Late projects incur continuing costs until they are completely finished. This diagram highlights the fact that costs keep accruing on projects until such time as they are completely implemented.

There are three areas in which the completion of a project is gauged. The first is delivery time. The second is development cost. The third is features implemented.

It is very common in our industry to focus on the delivery date. With the date tied to the development cost, many managers claim success by halting the project close to the scheduled end date, and thus close to the budgeted cost. They do this by deferring the implementation of features. Keep in mind that deferring features has affected the cost of the project. The user has now paid more for less, and the project is not complete. *The project costs will continue to accrue until the missing features are provided.*

MIS brings to the company to a position of no consequence. MIS needs to take proactive steps to change the way upper management perceives it. MIS must start marketing itself to upper management and MIS must take every opportunity to make upper management aware that it adds value to the company.

The main difficulty MIS encounters in this effort is its proxy representation to upper management. Several years ago there was a push to create a new position in MIS called the Chief Information Officer, or CIO. The reason behind this push was to make it possible for MIS to be directly represented to both the company president and the board of directors. The primary responsibility of the CIO is to represent the value that MIS provides to the company. If no CIO position exists, then MIS must use a proxy, typically the finance director, in the presentation of this value. Unfortunately, proxies are notorious for pushing their own perception of the MIS agenda rather than the actual MIS agenda. MIS organizations that are not represented by a CIO must work much harder to market themselves to upper management. Regardless of whether there is a CIO, the types of marketing are the same.

MIS must constantly present its accomplishments to upper management in the most objectively positive light possible. Then MIS must use its well-publicized creativity to interest upper management in viewing its accomplishments in the correct light. Remember that upper management does not think that MIS is worth the money. MIS must adopt an internal marketing strategy that addresses this issue. Following are some suggestions.

> **MIS Must Always Market Themselves to Upper Management. Good Looks and Charm Are Not Enough.**

When developing systems for user departments, MIS should insist that the user always be aware of the cost benefits of the new systems. MIS should then be sure to remind upper management that it is they, MIS, who are making this savings/revenue increase possible. When MIS takes steps to improve quality or reduce costs, MIS must remind upper management that it is MIS that is saving the company this money while still maintaining exceptional service levels. MIS must always be prepared to discuss its internal costs versus other MIS departments in the industry. Also reflecting directly on the issue of credibility, MIS must also stop taking credit for benefits from systems before they are actually implemented.

Finally, when there is no CIO available, MIS should try to publish its reports and metrics (as discussed below) to as wide an audience in the user organization and upper management as is politically possible. MIS must get out from under any disinterested or openly antagonistic proxy so it can present its own case to upper management.

Develop Service-Level Metrics

Service-level metrics are the only objective tool that MIS has available to defend its track record. Other political tools, such as presentations, establishing peer relationships among managers, and budgetary manipulations, are seldom used successfully by MIS (because MIS personnel are typically technocentric rather then sociocentric). Service-level metrics provide both the edge to a successful political defense and a tool for improving the performance of MIS. Objective measurements allow MIS to stand up and point to its successful efforts in a way that is both easy to do and highly effective. Note that the emphasis of service-level metrics is to demonstrate performance rather than to provide a means of improvement. This is appropriate because there is little solid evidence that traditional service-level metrics by themselves make an organization run better, and the newer service-level metrics are not yet widely used.

Service-level metrics consist of several categories of information. The first is on-time performance. This generally deals with advertising the status of the daily work—did the daily work get done on time? The second category is program/development quality, which deals with how error-free the application systems are. The third category is development performance: how often projects come in close to their original implementation date. The fourth category is user satisfaction. The final category is budget money.

On-Time Performance Metrics

The first category of metrics is used to prove that MIS delivers day-to-day services in a timely and reliable fashion. Most users perceive MIS functions as being bug-filled, often unavailable, and too slow to fulfill their business needs. On-time metrics prove these perceptions wrong.

On-line systems have two metrics that should be implemented: availability and response times. Charting the amount of downtime per day, week, month, and quarter demonstrates that the MIS services are delivered reliably. Charting the response times—minimum, maximum, average, and most common—demonstrates that MIS services are being delivered in a timely fashion. Consider these two metrics to be simple public relations, or even advertising. Since the users perceive that MIS is letting them down, MIS must always present these metrics as counter-arguments. Think of these two metrics as the dishwasher detergent ads of the television soaps. They provide little valuable information by themselves (assuming that the MIS services are being delivered in a reliable and timely fashion), but they reinforce the correct image of MIS in the eyes of the user communities.

Program/Development Effort Quality Metrics

This category of metrics has two uses: defending MIS against the charges of shoddy workmanship and providing a valuable feedback mechanism in the effort to improve the quality of the development efforts. There is no MIS organization in existence that is not responding to charges of bug-filled programs and systems. These charges range from the user interfaces being overly cumbersome to the individual programs being unusable because of problems. While some of the charges will always be true, most systems experience a very small level of problems when compared with their complexity.

All program errors that occur in view of the user need to be tracked by program, by programmer, by application subsystem, and by application system. These errors need to be tracked by length of time to fix; number of modules changed; and initial source of defect injection, i.e., requirements, specifications, design, or programming (Figure 8-2). Defect injection should never occur in the testing environment. The process of collecting these metrics is more time consuming and politically sensitive than that of the on-time metrics.

It Is Very Possible That Some Metrics May Be Written Into Law Over the Next Ten Years.

Recording these error statistics is a tedious job if management has not developed or does not enforce the procedures and policies supporting them. New process strategies such as ISO 9000 and the FDA's Best Good Manufacturing Procedures give new impetus to management support. However, the most important point to *always* keep in mind is that these procedures must not be followed mindlessly. The mindless collection of defect information or following of any procedures soon mutates into the excessive collection of valueless information and the excess fossification of development processes. Both remove precious time, money, and personnel resources from valid MIS functions.

The secondary value of these statistics and processes is the improvement in development efforts and results that *might*

Figure 8-2. 1.5 percent additional requirements per month.

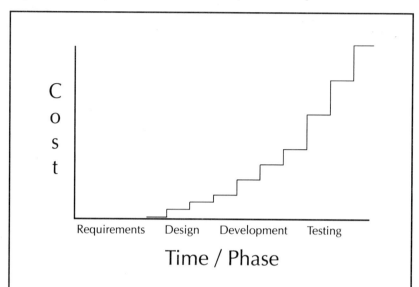

It has been shown empirically by organizations in the Function Fact Counting field that development projects that exceed twelve months in duration experience scope creep at the rate of 1.5 percent per month. This diagram demonstrates the effect of the scope creep on the cost of the project.

There is other empirical evidence (by Hewlett Packard, for example) that the project phase in which requirement changes are identified has a direct bearing on the cost of addressing those changed requirements. In fact, the industry figure is as follows. Additional requirements introduced in the design phase cost ten times more to address than if they were identified in the requirements phase. Requirements introduced in the programming (construction) phase cost ten times more than in the design phase. Ditto for testing versus programming, and production versus testing.

This diagram shows what happens to the cost if the cost factor is only three times instead of ten times. *Notice that the high costs come at the project end. This is why so many projects go from on time and within budget to late and over budget so quickly.*

occur. Because there is no direct link from the present to the future, it is impossible for the correction of a defect to lead to a guaranteed better development effort. Thus, one can only hope that more accurate metrics today will cause better systems tomorrow.

> ## Einstein Proved That Perception Is Reality.

The primary value of the statistics once again is based on their marketing value. Statistics on program errors and development quality should be used to demonstrate the effectiveness of the MIS organization. Using these statistics, it is possible to compare the MIS organization against industry standards. Remember that the decision to outsource MIS is based more on political considerations than on actual need. MIS must always address the real reason it was outsourced—company politics.

Development Performance Metrics

MIS projects usually entail large budgetary expenditures and long-term efforts. Contrast this with most company functions, which are repetitive in nature, low in complexity, and low in cost. High cost and long term are synonymous with high visibility. Development performance must be monitored to ensure that when projects are delivered on time, under budget, or both, MIS gets the appropriate credit. In MIS most projects are neither on time nor within budget. This is because of the level of complexity inherent in the end product. This complexity needs to be considered at every change of the development project schedule.

Metrics that mark development performance must be complete in both time orientation and scope. This means that these metrics must always take into account the date of the actions

versus the original schedule and must contain enough information to ensure that the metrics are not used out of context. Unfortunately, most of these metrics are used out of context
precisely because they do not encompass both the time and
scope aspects.

When a development effort starts to slide, it is imperative
that the metrics contain the reason for the slide. This reason will
almost always be associated with the realization of new requirements. In many cases, the MIS analyst will be blamed for not un-
covering these requirements at the right time in the project. It
should be noted, however, that in most of these cases the requirements were not actually known to the business function
that requested the new system. How can this be? It happens because the business functions MIS is interfacing with typically are
incapable of articulating all of the requirements in a timely fashion because they have never had to articulate them in the past.
In fact, their requirements were probably passed down through
the informal communications channels that exist in every organization, and the requirements do not exist in the mind of any
one individual but instead in the collective intelligence of the
business unit as a whole.

So it is imperative that MIS correctly categorize late requirements by the real reason they are late in being identified. This
could happen for one of three reasons. First, the analyst simply
got the requirements wrong; second, the analyst misunderstood
the requirements and was not corrected by the user organization; finally, the user organization did not realize there was an
additional requirement until it became apparent that the system,
as designed, would not work.

Once again the use of this information is primarily political.
The user organizations have spent years blaming MIS for late
and overly expensive projects, when two of the three causes of
the single largest reason for overruns are strictly their responsibility. These development quality metrics are needed to publi-
cize the value that MIS brings to the effort by ensuring that there
is an adequate and accurate assessment of responsibilities.

The bottom line on metrics is that they must be used to
demonstrate the value of MIS to the company and to dispel the

grossly inaccurate perception of MIS that prevails. MIS must take active measures to more correctly present itself to upper management.

User Satisfaction

MIS generally has no mechanism in place to measure or enhance user satisfaction. Some major software developers have focused on user satisfaction while others depend on simply appearing brilliant. Unfortunately for MIS there is usually nowhere to hide from user dissatisfaction.

Two of the largest companies in computing technologies, IBM and HP, have developed methods of measuring user satisfaction. Both these companies base their service-level metrics on these metrics. IBM in particular uses this as the first checkpoint in its improvement processes.

Budget Money

There is never enough budget money and regardless of how little MIS gets versus what it needs, there still should be metrics that benchmark the amount of money MIS is spending compared with other departments. Since MIS usually has a very large percentage of company expenditures, it is even more important that the budget monies be tracked and rated appropriately.

Many in management say that the common sense approach is to protect the budget first and provide service second. This is somewhat accurate but also self-defeating. Acquiring and keeping budget money is an art based on managing perception and fact. The fact is that MIS needs lots of money to fund its efforts. The general perception is that MIS does not need all of the monies it asks for. But MIS actually does need the monies it asks for, so metrics are required that demonstrate a relationship between both money and performance and money and value to the company.

Use of the financial techniques mentioned earlier in the chapter will significantly help MIS acquire its fair share of the budget dollars.

Rate People Objectively

Accurate assessment of personnel is very important for MIS. Since MIS personnel are highly paid compared with the rest of the company, it is imperative that each individual in MIS be worth the money. It is a fact that every MIS organization has some people who are not worth the money they are being paid. These people must be identified by management and either placed in more appropriate positions or encouraged to move on.

Many MIS managers do not want to be in a position of judging their employees. Many feel either that they are not capable of making that judgment or that making such a judgment is immoral. But making these judgments is an important part of managing people. Also, many *senior* people in an organization are senior simply because they have been around longer than everybody else, not because they have the skills for the position. The bottom line is that in twenty years many of these marginal personnel will be marginal managers. Then MIS will really have credibility, budget, delivery, and reliability problems.

Protecting the company in the long term and strengthening MIS in the short term requires objective analysis of personnel. Objective analysis is hard work for several reasons, starting with the requirement that management be objective. Objectivity requires appropriate metrics and a long-term commitment to hard work.

Managers must admit to themselves that they have favorites among the staff and that these favorites have been getting preferential treatment. This is not an astounding revelation; it happens in every department and at every level of management. Once this admission has been made, management should assess the reasons for the favoritism (for each individual) so they can be considered objectively.

> ## Recognize That Some People Are Really Good and Some People Are Really Bad and Lobby HR to Allow MIS to Act Accordingly.

Many metrics are available to MIS for rating people. Most of them are technical in nature. Programmers should be rated on their ability to generate error-free codes. Analysts should be rated on their ability to create error-free requirements. Designers should be rated on their ability to design error-free, high-performance, low-maintenance systems. Operations personnel should be rated on the reliability of their hardware and the proficiency of process execution. All of these ratings must take into account the complexity of the environment or the problems being addressed.

Establish a Migration to the Business Areas

Remember that even though the user community thinks MIS has a great deal of smart people in it, it still believes that MIS personnel are overpaid. Just as important is the fact the users do not understand what it takes to build and maintain computer systems and thus have no sympathy for the difficulties that MIS encounters. The consequence of these two facts is that none of the other departments consider MIS to be an ally. Instead MIS is considered an overpaid stumbling block to the user's computer system desires. Users firmly believe that they could do a much better job if only they could control MIS. Barring that control, they would just as soon see MIS removed from the company because they feel that this would mean there would be more money for their departments.

This perception is entirely false and needs to be rectified. Perceptions are based either on facts, as with an informed user, or marketing, as with heavily advertised products. The user community continually advertises the failures of MIS to itself as one way of managing company politics. MIS, needless to say, is generally not capable of understanding company politics. Therefore, MIS cannot count on advertising to improve how it is perceived by the user community. Instead, MIS must take concrete steps to improve the perception of value that the user community experiences. The most effective method is to utilize the lateral communication lines that permeate all companies.

The best way to demonstrate to the user communities that MIS is valuable is to place MIS personnel directly into their areas. This can be accomplished in several ways. First, the MIS business analysts for each user group should be officed with the users. Second, any development efforts should be officed with the users. Third, maintenance teams should be officed with the users. Lastly, MIS personnel who are tired of the stress of MIS should be encouraged to accept senior positions within the user areas.

Note that with the exception of the last suggestion, encouraging staff migration to user areas, MIS is not giving up control of staff. Instead, MIS is improving communication with the user groups via close physical contact. These actions are designed to break down any *us versus them* barriers that are usually present.

MIS Staff Is the Best Resource Most Companies Have. When They Leave MIS, Place Them Where They Can Continue to Help MIS and the Company.

Placing MIS personnel in user areas has the following effect on perception. First, MIS people generally have a wider view of the functions that the user area performs. This is a consequence of the need to integrate the user's systems with the other systems within the company. Second, MIS personnel understand the effort and problems that are typically encountered during development and maintenance efforts. This leads to a more realistic level of expectations in the user area. Third, because MIS personnel are highly paid compared with the other department personnel, the migration of MIS personnel demonstrates to the user community that its areas are both valuable and attractive to others within the company. This in turn raises the users' self-esteem and allows them to interface with MIS in a more open and understanding manner.

Epilogue

Consider the following quotation and think about it in terms of MIS and the overall company welfare.

> "Mercenaries and auxiliaries are useless and dangerous. If a prince bases the defense of his state on mercenaries he will never achieve stability or security."
>
> From *The Prince* by Machiavelli

Many executives already feel that MIS is staffed by mercenaries. This feeling is based on the higher wages MIS personnel command and the fact that MIS personnel are always in demand at other companies. Naturally these executives are wrong in this judgment. MIS employees are as loyal as upper management allows them to be.

For those companies that rely on the MIS function for survival, outsourcing is a slow death by suicide. For those who are outsourcing only the support or back-office functions, outsourcing may not be so bad. Regardless of the functions being outsourced, it is wise to keep the advice from *The Prince* in mind.

Appendix A

The Outsourcer Sales Pitch

Marketing outsourcing services consists of selling the client management on the benefits of giving up control, responsibility, and ownership of client assets. The language of outsourcing defines some of these benefits, while the act of marketing the services defines others. The following discussion considers the most common selling points and strategies.

Note that while the premise of this book is outsourcing agreements gone bad, not all do so. While the basis for this appendix is the articulation of counter-arguments to the outsourcer's marketing pitch, this does not mean that the outsourcer's marketing pitch is misleading or fraudulent. Clients that do not challenge every statement or claim made by the outsourcer are not doing their job properly. When an outsourcer makes a claim of benefits it is imperative that the client investigate the validity and the appropriateness of the claim to their needs.

Outsourcer claims that are invalid need to be rejected immediately. Otherwise, the claim will be implicitly accepted throughout the remainder of the negotiation activities. A claim that is not appropriate for or has no value to the client must also be rejected immediately; otherwise, the outsourcer will expect to be *paid* (via higher prices for other services) for its value.

Consider this. The value of an outsourcing agreement is based largely on the perceived value of the services to the client.

By removing claims that have no value to the client, the perceived value of the package will decrease, as will the final package price.

The Good

Outsourcing has benefits for many organizations. The following are marketing points that are very strong benefactors to the client organizations.

Asset Transfer

Point. Removing assets from the client books can provide a financial benefit. Accounting rules and tax laws can be manipulated to improve the financial position of a client, not just on paper but in actuality. Thus the assumption of these assets by the outsourcer is a serious benefit.

Counterpoint. Accounting rules and tax laws change from year to year. What is a benefit one year may be a detriment the next year. Transferring older generation resources to the outsourcer might also impede its ability to provide adequate service in later years.

Cash Buy-In

Point. Outsourcers that buy into the customer's business provide much needed cash.

Counterpoint. While no one can argue the benefits of cash on hand, there are two ancillary points that must be considered before signing the deal. First, the buy-in price must be competitive and not discounted. In other words, the client must sell out for a good price. Second, the buy-in should be looked at as a loan with an attached *interest* rate. This interest rate must also be competitive. And like any good loan, the terms should be settled in advance and constant throughout the term of the loan. In other words, buy-ins with balloon payments at the end or nonsimple interest calculations must be avoided.

Does this analogy with a consumer loan sound confusing? The reason for the analogy is this. When an outsourcer buys into the client he is doing so with the client's money. No outsourcer is going to buy into a client for less money than will be earned over the course of the agreement. Thus, it is really a loan that the client pays back over the life of the agreement, with interest. On top of this payback are the other charges for the outsourcing service itself. It is necessary to view a buy-in situation as a second transaction, distinct from the actual charges for the outsourcing services.

Expertise in Technology

Point. Outsourcers deal with the technology involved in the outsourcing agreement as their primary line of business. They not only have a high level of experience in the technology business; they also have management experience in this same area. Dealing with an expert makes sense. Experts know the issues, the concerns, and the players—who can get what done, for how much, and how long it will take.

Counterpoint. Outsourcer expertise is in the technology side of the outsourcing and not the business side. Indeed, for business expertise, the outsourcer either has to go back to the client and take staff from them or go to the client's competitors for staffing. In either case, the outsourcer is sadly lacking in the client's business knowledge.

While technology expertise is important, business expertise is more important. If an IS development group is being outsourced, the client will probably receive poor service from the beginning, although it will not appear poor to the casual observer. The reason for this is that most cost and schedule overruns in MIS development projects are associated with the inadequate understanding of user requirements. Because they are not experts in the client's business, outsourcers face an immediate obstacle in determining user requirements. Or they may determine lots of user requirements but not understand the importance of each one and thus develop a product that does not adequately address the user's needs. The problems resulting from this lack of understanding will usually show up late in the development cycle when it is very expensive, in both time and money, to fix them.

The Bad

Outsourcing marketing efforts include several attributes that are actually worthless or detrimental to the client organization. They make sense upon initial presentation, but closer looks prove their expense.

Best of Breed

Point. This marketing phrase is used to emphasize the talent of the employees of the outsourcer. Because the outsourcer specializes in data processing services, it needs to attract and keep the best people available. Clients get the advantage of this attribute because they either cannot afford to pay for this caliber of people or they cannot keep these people on staff.

    Counterpoint. Outsourcers draw their staff from the same candidate pool as the customer. Outsourcer salaries are competitive, but typically not higher than the client's. The outsourcer environment is more interesting than the client organization when changes are taking place. However, a changing outsourcer environment is bad for the client (see "The Ugly" below), so the net effect of the outsourcer being an interesting place to work is definitely a minus for the client. Finally, facing up to the obvious, the outsourcer must admit that most of its staff comes from the client, so how can it be better?

Full-Time Equivalents (Unnamed Support Personnel)

Point. Outsourcers couple the best of breed argument with the use of unnamed personnel for client support. The premise is that the client will get some full-time equivalent (FTE) people for each category and the right to draw on additional FTEs when needed. The justification for this technique is twofold. First, the outsourcer staff is so good that they are interchangeable on a moment's notice. Second, this allows the outsourcer to keep the cost to the client low, thus giving the client the cost savings it seeks.

Counterpoint. The best of breed argument was discredited above, so the people involved in providing services to the client are no better than they were when the service was in-house. Additionally, people are not *plug and play*. The fact is that anyone given a new task has an orientation time penalty that must be paid before the person can be productive. On a large project, system, or effort, this will usually be a minimum of two weeks (based on the author's experience) and will usually stretch to months. Prior to that time the benefits of the plug and play person are minimal and are usually restricted to special case contributions. In fact, contributions made before the person is fully oriented can easily be damaging in the long run instead of being beneficial.

Plug and play personnel keep the outsourcer's cost down, but also increase the uncertainty of the efforts undertaken by the outsourcer.

Plug and play personnel increase the training costs associated with a system (Figure A-1). The training time is based on people, not partial people. If it takes two weeks to train a person, you cannot select three people and train each in three-and-a-third days (3.333... × 3 = 10). It actually takes six man-weeks to train three people at two weeks per person. Why is it necessary to make this point so strongly? Most clients lose sight of the fact that each person used in an FTE environment must be trained. Thus an outsourcer using five people to provide one FTE has five times the training cost (and the client must pay this expense, either in direct dollars, bad design, bad programming, or bad service).

Figure A-1. Training costs for full-time equivalents.

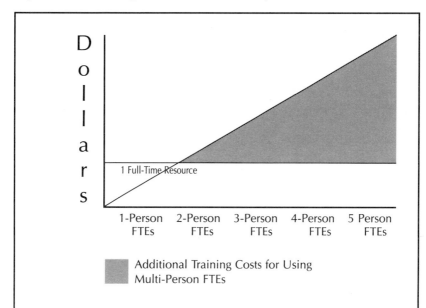

This diagram shows the increase in training costs associated with using Full-Time Equivalents (FTEs) instead of dedicated resources. The shaded area represents the increased costs associated with using more than one person to make up an FTE.

While the point is obvious, it is always overlooked. The outsourcer has no incentive to remind the client that personnel are not interchangeable. The client usually has other aspects of the outsourcing contract on their mind.

The use of FTEs instead of dedicated support personnel virtually guarantees that the outsourcing effort will fail, and quickly. Why is this? Consider the precedent being set when it costs two, three, or four times as much to train the support personnel as anticipated. Or, if the training costs are not spent, consider the loss of expertise and additional problems caused by not adequately training the support personnel. *Using FTEs is a lose-lose situation.*

Economies of Scale

Point. Outsourcers claim that they benefit from economies of scale when it comes to purchasing equipment and services. They also claim that they are able to provide more cost-effective solutions through the effective reuse of existing resources. This statement is true under some circumstances. For instance, a help desk function supporting PC users running industry standard consumer software can benefit from economies of scale.

Counterpoint. Outsourcers rarely get significantly better terms on their mainframe equipment purchases/leases than most clients. There may have been a savings in software licensing fees in the past, but software developers have adjusted their fee schedules so that clients using outsourcers pay the same licensing fees they would pay if they had their own equipment. From a cost standpoint, it is hard to support this argument.

The Ugly

Some marketing strategies are simply hard to swallow after they have been shown to be misleading time and time again. While they are good for the outsourcer, they are bad for the client.

Marketing to Upper Management Only

Point. Several major outsourcers make a point of marketing their services only to executive management. They are introduced to the MIS organization only after upper management has decided to do the outsourcing. When they get to MIS, the outsourcers are not offering a service; they are implementing a fiat.

Counterpoint. How can an outsourcer know more about a client's business needs than the internal MIS organization? They can't. A two-week study, or even a six-month-long study, cannot provide both the data and the wisdom needed to adequately assess the needs of a complex organization. Given that it is impossible for an outsourcer to understand an existing MIS organization on anything other than the most superficial level, how can it in good conscience offer itself as the solution to a client's problem? In fact, how do they even know the client has a problem?

Maybe upper management thinks a problem exists, and that is why the outsourcer was called in to do an assessment. If upper management thinks it has a problem, it is because it hired, or supported, or kept the managers in MIS who are having the problem.

Maintaining and Protecting Existing Client Staff

Point. Outsourcers often receive a transfer of employees from the client when the contract takes effect. When this occurs, there is usually a clause in the contract requiring the outsourcer to keep these employees on their staff for a period of from six months to one year.

Counterpoint. The public reason for this clause is the protection of the client's newly departed employees. The real reason is to protect the knowledge base represented by the ex-employees. In theory this works, but in practice it does not. What usually occurs is that once the outsourcing agreement is made public, there is an immediate migration of employees to other jobs. Within six months after the agreement has been executed, usually fewer than 50 percent of the client's employees are still employed by the outsourcer. In some cases the percentage drops to as low as 25 percent. The client's ex-employees are not available to maintain the knowledge base. The outsourcer has to develop its own in-house expertise, which usually takes substantially longer than six months.

Even worse, most outsourcers have no incentive to keep, and lots of incentive to terminate, these employees past the contracted period. And if an employee terminates of his own free will before the contract period expires, it is not held against the outsourcer. Thus, the outsourcer has both no incentive to keep the client's ex-employee; it also has no incentive to keep the client's ex-employee happy.

Outsourcer Maintaining State-of-the-Art Facilities

Point. Outsourcers need state-of-the-art (SOTA) facilities to attract and retain clients. Without SOTA facilities, client needs cannot be satisfied and service levels will suffer. This SOTA positioning allows the outsourcer to respond quickly and professionally to any client need.

Counterpoint. Many outsourcers take over the client's data processing facilities. These facilities are not SOTA. Upgrading existing facilities is an expensive proposition. If it were cheap the client would have already done it. The successful service bureaus of the past always ran with older generation technology. Older generation technology provided them with low-cost hardware and software.

An outsourcer will typically acquire newer generation equipment, possibly even SOTA equipment, during the acquisition of a new client. This acquisition will benefit all of the existing clients from a hardware standpoint, but as noted earlier in the book, it will generally result in a decreased service level to the existing clients as time goes on. Thus, SOTA is not even a dream for most outsourcers.

Appendix B

Companies That Should Be Outsourced

While the premise of this book does not advocate outsourcing as a solution for all MIS organizations, it does recognize that some companies may actually benefit from outsourcing. Three key areas of an MIS organization that should be assessed for potential outsourcing are distributed computing and networking, data processing operations, and application development. There is a possibility that all three of these areas should be outsourced. However, the probability is that at least one of the areas will benefit.

Distributed computing and networking would benefit if the outsourcing partner's expertise in technology is greater than the company considering outsourcing. Another benefit may be derived if the outsourcer has standards, policies, and procedures regarding network configuration tools, security, and version control.

Data processing operations is probably the most efficient area within an MIS organization, mainly because it is the most visible area within the company. The nature of operations is a production environment that is repeatable. Night after night the opportunity arises to improve the production process. While the users are involved in providing requirements to the application development organizations, it is operations that represents MIS. If users experience slow response times or high unavailability, it is immediately associated with operations, not the specific application. This is logical since the user sits in front of a terminal and has expectations about the capability of the system in relation to the hardware that is the direct interface to the user. Operations is a spin-off of the service bureaus whose profitability was based on efficiency of processing millions of transactions within specified time frames. The service bureau concepts were brought back in-house as data volumes increased and demands for shorter turnaround time increased.

The application development area is also highly viable for outsourcing. The majority of the budget overruns occur in application development. While this is also a highly repeatable area, little is done to capture historical data that can be used to improve the next development effort. An outsourcer with standards, processes, and methodologies can significantly improve the application development area.

Company Profile

The following depicts the profile of a company that should be outsourced. The profile is valid for each of the three key areas that should be assessed for outsourcing. While a company may not have all of the attributes profiled here, each of these requires attention. This can be accomplished independent of an outsourcing agreement; however, a concerted effort must be made to rectify the vulnerability posed by the implications of these attributes.

Lack of Standards, Policies, and Procedures

Standards, policies, and procedures make up the cement that binds the infrastructure of an MIS organization. Most organizations will espouse that they have standards, policies, and procedures, but in reality these are usually not documented, not followed, and not controlled to ensure compliance.

Lack of Processes and Methodologies

Like standards, policies, and procedures, processes and methodologies are seldom defined and followed in an MIS organization. These are the building blocks of the infrastructure. Processes establish the protocols by which MIS will interact with the client, external vendors, and customers and the interaction of the MIS departments, such as operations, development, and security. Methodologies are the "how to." These define the set order of activities—they are road maps for the roles and responsibilities of all those touched by MIS, including MIS itself. The majority of companies follow some processes, otherwise the nightly production would not get done nor would any enhancements or technology upgrades occur. However, the key here is repeatability and consistency. Is there any manner by which the processes can be leveraged to improve the efficiency and increase productivity? Without a defined process or methodology to baseline against, there can be no measure of improvement.

Poor Documentation

Documentation is a four-letter word in most companies. Documentation is consistently compromised to make project deadlines. Over the years, the majority of the core functionality is supported by individuals who are domain experts. The vulnerability here is that the organization becomes personality driven. "If only I had the right people, I could get this project done." "If only I had the right people, I could improve the production cycle." These are excuses many managers give themselves.

MIS knowledge becomes exclusive to an elite few. The information is disseminated on an as-needed basis. The individuals with domain expertise become the most valuable commodities.

Lack of Change Control

Change control encompasses requirements specifications, software configuration management, and testing. Symptoms of the lack of these controls are scope creep during projects and intro-duction of new bugs into the production environment. Change control, by its very nature, implies removal of authority. Control is exactly that: project controls and control of the production en-vironment. Testing is the gateway to production and is often viewed as a roadblock, a necessary evil. However, like docu-mentation, testing is often compromised to meet a project dead-line. Change control is an effective means of managing projects and protecting the production environment.

Lack of Metrics and Measurements

Without metrics and measurements an organization can never determine the value added to the business and can never deter-mine improvements and justify costs. Metrics and measure-ments enable an organization to better estimate and schedule work. Each year the budget process becomes more arduous as more companies require MIS organizations to become profit-and-loss centers.

Eroding Skill Sets

Employee training and development is another area compro-mised to make project deadlines and to meet budget objectives. Often, training is used as a perk for a job well done. However, the focus of the organization is usually on those considered the firefighters, those employees who are always there to help when there is a production problem. The organization rarely focuses on the fire preventers. These are the individuals who manage to document, develop project plans, and look for means of opti-mizing the processes. Training and development must be as-sessed in relation to the core competencies to which the MIS organization aspires. Training and development must be viewed as a means to be proactive, to leverage skills to better meet busi-ness needs.

Lack of Domain Experts

Lack of domain experts often is coupled with eroding skill sets and is a symptom of a lack of redundancy to increase a knowledge base. The expertise erodes over time as personnel move on to new areas and have not documented their areas of expertise. It is not uncharacteristic for personnel to be prevented from making a career move because no one else knows the particular area of a system process or application.

Domain experts acquire a breadth and depth usually beyond what is normally required because of documentation. The crux of this is that the domain experts become the firefighters.

Lack of Redundancy to Increase Knowledge Base

Most organizations do not have the time, nor do they have the additional resources required to increase the knowledge base. While these excuses have become the norm, the nature of the environment has changed drastically over last five years. New technologies are introduced that tempt personnel in an MIS organization to seek greener pastures. With the introduction of outsourcing, personnel recognize themselves as valuable commodities, and the message has been sent loud and clear that the company can easily replace them through an outsourcing agreement.

The loyalties once mutually perceived have been eroded with outsourcing. Is this such a bad thing? Personnel have gained a level of confidence not previously recognized, and the company recognizes that it must raise its expectations with regard to personnel performance.

Appendix C

Metrics That Can Gauge Service Levels

Metrics are numbers that are generated through an objective process of observation. Metrics are repeatable and nonmagical and can be generated by anyone capable of following directions. Metrics are impartial to the political orientation of the generator. That said, clients need to watch out how metrics are used. While the generation of the metrics is mostly mechanical, the interpretation of them is often done through the use of snake oil and politically colored glass.

Clients need metrics to challenge the claims of the outsourcers and to monitor the service level of the outsourcers. The metrics used by the client must be designed to support these goals. Choosing metrics without focusing on these needs provides the client with no value.

Metrics can be generated that measure overall service levels, individual problem areas, and even staff expertise. All of these are service-level related. The following metrics can provide a starting point for the client.

Measuring Overall Service Levels

The single most important metric for in-house or outsourced work is the service level being provided. This metric measures either the rate of on-time processing, the actual versus budgeted cost, the actual versus scheduled development time, or any combination of the above. Generally the service level is reflected in the attitude of the users. Low service levels usually create surly and wary user communities. High service levels embody themselves as self-confident and smug user attitudes. Of course, low service levels also push users to demand changes, while high service levels create a desire to maintain the status quo. Service levels are always a combination of the amount of work being performed, the quality of the work, and the cost of the work. Money plays a large part in this metric.

Service Level—The Easiest Way

On-time delivery, at the budgeted cost and with the requested functionality, is the best measure of the service level. Unfortunately there are few well-defined methods to calculate this metric. The formula presented here is one of the simplest to be found. As a consequence, it can be ambiguous in its value. However, if it is applied uniformly, with a conservative view of its value, it can be very helpful to those organizations that have no existing metric.

Unweighted Service Level = ((Number of On-Time Processes / Number of Processes) + (Budgeted Expenses / Actual Expenses) + (Projected Durations of Projects / Actual Durations of Projects)) / 3

If everything is going perfectly this metric will return a value of 1. Numbers lower than 1 indicate that some areas of service need to be improved. A value of .9 or less indicates there are real problems with the organization being rated.

If this metric is used for a year or more, it can indicate trends. For instance, if the metric is dropping, then the organization's service level is decreasing and steps should be taken to remedy the problem areas. If the metric is rising, the organization is improving the way it performs its work.

Service Level—A Slightly Better Way

The previous service level formula assumed that all things were equal, and this is normally not the case. Each organization has different priorities based on the needs of the user community. For some companies, on-time completion of the production work is much more important than actual costs or on-time delivery of new development. For other companies, the opposite is true. One easy way to compensate for these differences in priorities is to place a weight in front of each of the previous terms. This weight would be used to specify the relative importance of the term to the organization.

Weighted Service Level = (On-Time Weight × (Number of On-Time Processing / Number of Processes) + Budget Weight × (Budgeted Expenses / Actual Expenses) + On-Time Delivery Weight × (Projected Durations of Projects / Actual Durations of Projects)) / 3

By scaling each of the individual terms by its weight, the organization can get a more realistic indication of service level from the equation. Unfortunately, the interpretation of the results is more complicated. This metric can take any value between zero and (On-Time Weight + Budget Weight + On-Time Delivery Weight) / 3. But the same criteria as above, stated as a ratio instead of an absolute, can be used. Therefore, if the metric return is less than .9 of the maximum value, then the organization has serious problems. This metric can also be tracked over time.

Measuring Problem Areas

Several areas are traditionally problem areas in an organization. These are low hardware availability, late reports or processing, on-line system downtime, and late development delivery. These are the classic problem areas, and in an outsourced environment they can become major problems very quickly. Metrics that map onto these areas can be used to identify problems before they become too big. This can only be done through the consistent use of the metrics over long periods of time. Snapshots cannot be used effectively if an organization wants to keep problems from occurring; they can only be used to react to existing problems. One word of warning: Many times these metrics are available for review, but management either forgets it has them or refuses to believe them (for one reason or another).

Hardware Availability—The Easiest Way

In this world of client/server processing, especially when it is defined to include the workstations at everyone's desk, hardware availability becomes very hard to compute. However, two things are valid regardless of the environment. First, the more people who use a resource, the more important it is. Second, the more a resource costs, the more important it is. This first metric ignores both of those and simply gives a percentage of downtime for the entire equipment base.

Hardware Availability = SUM (Time Available / Time Needed) / Number of Items of Equipment

This metric requires that each piece of equipment be identified and its individual downtime tracked. An example would be a user organization with 20 workstations and one server where the employees work 40 hours per week. The Time Needed term would be 40 hours for each piece of equipment. If one workstation went down for 4 hours during the week, that workstation would have an availability of .9 and the rest would have an availability of 1. The Hardware Availability for the group as a whole would be ((20 x (40/40)) + (36/40)) / 21 or .995.

Most people can already see the problem with this metric. If the Hardware Availability is .995 then no one can possibly complain about downtime. But if it had been the server that was down for 4 hours during that week, 20 people would have been inconvenienced instead of 1, and this metric will not show that impact.

Hardware Availability—
People / Hour Impact (CMI)

This metric starts with the Hardware Availability equation mentioned above and modifies it to weight the result by the number of people impacted by the problem. If the times are given in minutes, these equations can give the Client Minutes of Interruption. It has been shown that in medium-size companies (300 to 600 employees) LANs that experience 5 percent downtime cost over $4 million per year in lost work time.

Hardware Availability = (SUM (Number of People Dependent On Equipment x (Time Available / Time Needed)) / Number of Items of Equipment) / (SUM (Number of People Dependent On Equipment) / Number of Items of Equipment)

Using the same example of one server and 20 workstations, and the same downtime situations (a workstation for 4 hours or the server for 4 hours) the metric delivers the following results:

One workstation down for 4 hours gives a result of .9975 for availability.

One server down for 4 hours gives a result of .95.

While .9975 is an acceptable availability rate, .95 is not, because it indicates that 5 percent of your employees' time is affected by hardware failures. Thus, this metric provides a better indication of hardware availability than the first.

This metric can also be modified to use cost as a factor rather than the number of people involved. To do this, substitute the cost of the resource for the number of people using it.

Client Minutes of Interruption (CMI) = SUM (Number of People Dependent On Equipment x Time Not Available)

While much simpler than the Hardware Availability equation, this equation gives a much stronger statement of impact.

Report Availability—The Easiest Way

Even in this world of on-line systems and Internet connectivity, daily reports are still an important part of the business world. These reports, which used to be delivered solely on paper, now come on microfiche, microfilm, 3270 images, and downloaded report files. Generally, their major attributes are that they deliver massive amounts of information on a regular basis. Examples of these reports could be the Friday night report, the payroll report, and the quarterly report. Their major import is that when they are not available on time, some function, either major or minor, cannot be performed, and employees are sitting idle or money is being lost.

Unweighted Report Availability = SUM (1 if Report Available On Time, 0 if Report Not Available On Time)/ Number of Reports

Using this metric, if 1 report out of 20 is late, the metric will return .95 indicating that 95 percent of the reports are on time. Once again, this metric is not sensitive to the importance of the individual reports. Nonetheless, most companies can use a metric of this type to indicate report availability.

Report Availability—A Better Metric

The following metric weights the report availability based on either the number of people affected, the monies placed in jeopardy, or the political fallout of each report. This metric is more powerful than the previous metric because it can be used to more fully describe the effect of the downtime.

Weighted Report Availability = SUM (Value of On-Time Delivery × 1 if Report Available On Time, 0 if Report Not Available On Time)/ SUM (Value of On-Time Delivery of Report)

In this metric, the value of a report is presented in the number of people affected, the monies placed in jeopardy, or the political fallout. The value returned is a number between zero and one, where one is 100 percent availability. Reports that have greater value have a greater impact on the result of the metric. Once again, this metric should be run on a continuous basis so that problem areas can be corrected before too much damage is done.

On-Line Availability—The Easiest Way

Back when all on-line systems were mainframe-based, on-line availability was easy to track. If the host was down everyone was out of work. Today's client/server and distributed processing environments complicate the tracking of the impact of on-line downtime. Instead of tracking just one resource, each individual resource must be tracked. Once again, the following metric simplifies the assessment of the impact of downed resources:

Unweighted On-line Availability = SUM (Duration Resource Is Available/ Duration Resource Needs to Be Available)/Number of Resources

Regardless of the number of resources in use, this metric will generate a value that can be used to grade availability. Thus, if only one host is in use this metric works fine, or if twenty servers are involved this metric also works.

On-Line Availability—A Better Way

The following metric applies a value to each resource and uses that value to scale the resulting metric value. Each resource is assigned a value based on either the number of people impacted, the monies at risk, or the political ramifications of its downtime. This metric provides a more accurate reflection of the impact of downtime on an organization.

Weighted On-line Availability = SUM ((Duration Resource Is Available/ Duration Resource Needs to Be Available) x Value of Resource) / SUM (Value of Resource)

The benefit of this metric is that the true impact of an individual resource's downtime, as seen in relation to the other resources, is reflected in the metric's value. The problem with this technique is that the amount of data necessary to make this metric truly reflective is large and probably requires some sort of automated downtime tracking system.

Development Delivery—The Easiest Way

It comes as no surprise to most people who interface with MIS that many development projects are delivered late and over budget. A natural side effect of this is that these projects usually come in with reduced functionality compared with the original feature set. The deferral of features is a time-honored method of delivering a product *on time.* Many of the major software companies are masters of delivering products that are missing features. Unfortunately for the receivers of these products, few people are in a position to actually say what features are missing, what they cost, and how late the product will actually be. (See Figures C-1 and C-2.)

This metric is designed to provide a quick snapshot of the development efforts underway or just completed. Note that this metric is trivial to compute and open to much interpretation. If it is used, it must be backed with a large amount of documentation.

Unweighted Development Timeliness = SUM (Actual Project Duration of Project) / SUM (Scheduled Project Duration of Project)

The result of this metric is a number from 0 to N indicating the average project duration. Values greater than 1 indicate that the projects generally come in late. A value of 2 indicates that the average project comes in at twice the duration than scheduled. Since this metric is an unweighted average, it can easily hide the effect of late projects or exaggerate the lateness of projects.

(text continues on page 152)

Figure C-1. Cost per function.

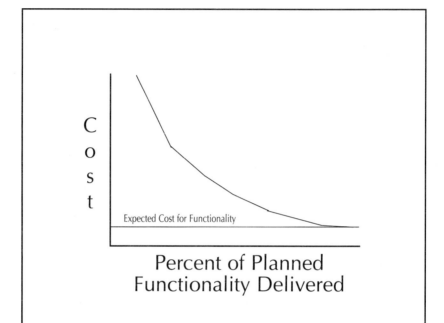

This diagram demonstrates the cost per function on a project when adjusted for missing functionality. Note that as the percentage of functionality actually implemented in a project increases, the average cost per function decreases.

The intent of this diagram is to emphasize the fact that many project managers depend on users not realizing that they paid way more for their resulting system than they ever imagined.

Using this diagram in an outsourced environment alerts the client to the real costs of projects that do not deliver as initially promised.

The cost per function demonstrated in this diagram can be used to forecast the cost of putting the missing functions into the project.

Figure C-2. Traditional cost curves.

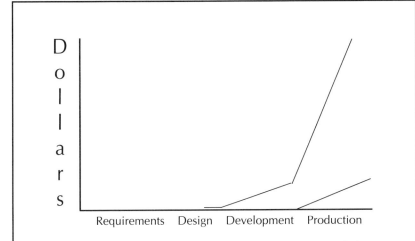

Note That Costs Are Not Visible Until Project Nears Completion

This diagram highlights two major project attributes. If the project experiences scope creep, there will be an explosion of cost toward the end of the project. If functionality is deferred until after the project is officially complete, it will cost from tens to thousands of times more to implement than if it had not been deferred.

Every effort must be made to stop scope creep from occurring. If additional requirements can be prevented from seeping into the project, both the explosion in cost before project completion and the expensive retrofitting of functionality can be avoided.

Project managers who allow their staff to start building the system before the requirements have been completely identified are setting themselves up for failure. This failure starts showing up once the project is 80 percent complete. Once 90 percent of the scheduled project duration has been reached, it will be obvious that functions will have to be jettisoned if the projected end-date is to be met.

Development Delivery—Include Costing Data

Including money in the metric provides a better guide to the development profile of the organization. Money is the unbiased metric of a capitalistic society. This metric uses money amounts that are not adjusted for inflation. Thus, long-running projects have a smaller impact on the metric than shorter projects.

Unweighted Development Cost = SUM (Actual Project Cost of Project) / SUM (Scheduled Project Cost of Project)

Using money instead of time provides the first metric capable of giving value judgments to a delivery profile. There is still much missing from this metric, but for a quick snapshot of an organization's performance this metric will suffice.

Development Delivery—Include Costing Data and Missing Functions

Users would not ask for features unless they thought they were valuable. When the project was scheduled these features were included along with the money to fund them. Therefore, when a project comes in late (or on time) with functions missing, but the original budget is spent (or overspent), these missing features need to be evaluated. The original schedule and budget should contain enough information to determine the estimated cost of the missing features. These amounts need to be added back into the actual project cost to accurately reflect the cost of the project.

Development Cost = SUM (Actual Cost of Project + SUM (Cost of Each Missing Feature)) / SUM (Scheduled Project Cost of Project)

This metric now provides the most complete project cost ratio that can be obtained with simple numbers. Values greater than 1.0 indicate that projects are coming in over budget. The extensions required to make this metric usable in an academic environment include the conversion of costs to NPVs and the inclusion of the value to the users of the missing features. One additional modification might be to scale the cost of the missing features by the ratio of the actual cost versus the budgeted cost, this being justified by the thought that if the delivered functions were, for example, 20 percent more expensive, the missing features would also be 20 percent more expensive if they had been delivered.

Measuring Staff Expertise

Staff expertise is half of the foundation on which most outsourcers base their sales pitch (cost saving is the other half). Clients need an objective way to compare staff with the outsourcer. Using the following metric allows the client to say "Yes, the outsourcer has better staff than us," or "No, we have better staff than the outsourcer." Most clients never make this effort because they have no method to compare. Another point that must be made is that most client staff transferred to the outsourcer will terminate within the first year, so the use of this metric must take this into account.

Staff Expertise—The Easiest Way

When a high-tech firm bids on a project, such as building a space station, one of the things they do is count PhDs. Commercial businesses rarely have PhDs on their staffs, so a more pragmatic approach needs to be taken. The following formula computes the number of man-years of expertise on the staff.

$$Unweighted\ Expertise = SUM\ (Number\ of\ man\text{-}years\ of\ experience\ per\ employee)$$

This metric provides the raw data from which the client can start making comparisons. Arguments can be made, for example, that the client has 500 man-years of experience while the outsourcer has only 200 man-years. Management can interpret this in one of two ways. Management can decide that MIS is overstaffed and thus justify the outsourcing decision. Or, it could decide that the outsourcer just does not have the capacity to support the client.

This metric can be used at any time before the outsourcing decision is made, after the outsourcing decision is made, or when the insourcing is taking place.

The problem with this metric is it can be used by either side and the smoothest talker will probably be the determinant of who profited most from its use. To negate this ambiguity, several of these numbers could be generated for different categories. The first would be the number of man-years of business experience. This would tell you who has the most solid *business experience* (instead of data processing experience). The second could be the total man-years from the first metric divided by the total from the second. This *ratio* could be used to demonstrate the overall strength or weakness of a staff.

Staff Expertise—By Category

This metric can be used to determine if the right number of resources of each type is available. It is used in conjunction with job titles to show whether the staff is graded appropriately and to show whether the right proportion of employees is at each staff level.

Grade Profile = Each Grade (COUNT (Number of employees in the grade))

This metric creates a histogram, as demonstrated in Figure C-3. Each column in this table represents the number of employees in a given salary grade. Ideally an MIS staff should have many employees at the lower grades and fewer staff as the grades increase.

Salary levels can be mapped onto a similar histogram. Job types can also be mapped onto a similar histogram. The three

Figure C-3. Positions within grade.

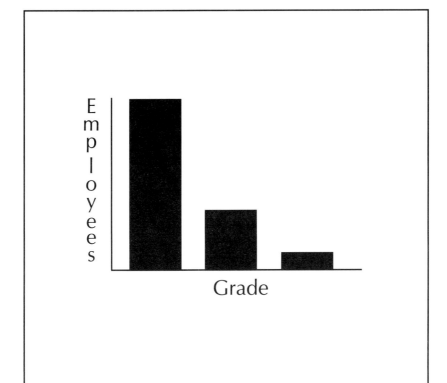

The most important feature of this diagram is the observation that as the grade increases, the number of employees in the grade decreases in a non-linear fashion. This is the traditional distribution of employee skills.

When this chart is compared against salary levels, they usually look exactly alike. But the implications of this chart are subtle and very important. By bottom-loading the organizational skills, the company and outsourcer are placing constraints on their ability to perform work. Maybe it is time to recast the distribution of skills within these organizations.

histograms should have a similar shape. If the histograms do not match, then the staff characteristics are out of sync with the needs of the organization.

Comparing the client versus outsourcer histograms will provide a revealing look at the capacities of the two organizations. Remember that the outsourcer's histograms must be scaled if they use FTEs (plug and play employees). If the outsourcer is proposing to use two or three people per FTE, then the man-years of those employees must be scaled through some mechanism. Unfortunately there is no mechanism available to do this, so a simple solution is to average the man-years per FTE and then divide again by the number of people making up the FTE. While this sounds harsh, it may be appropriate, since the outsourcer will only be providing a portion of a person at any one time.

Weighted Grade Profile = Each Grade (COUNT (Number of employees in the grade) x SUM (Number of man-years of experience per employee in the grade)

This metric creates a histogram that is scaled by the relative experience of the staff in each grade. This can be used to demonstrate the approximate strength of the personnel in the corresponding grades. Once again, this metric can also be modified to show strength in the business function by scaling by the man-years of business experience of each staff member.

Appendix D

Improving Organizational Efficiency

If an organization is a candidate for outsourcing because it truly is inefficient or impossible to control, the advice in this appendix should go a long way toward removing that impetus. None of these suggestions is a silver bullet, but each has value in and of itself. Implementing these suggestions is the hard part. Typically organizations that are inefficient or hard to control lack discipline and structure. Without discipline it is very hard to build structure. Structure is what makes efficient organizations.

Place the Organization Under a Related Functional Area

The classic example of data processing organizations being mismanaged starts with their being controlled by another department. While it is true that in the past DP systems were mostly related to managing the company books, that situation changed years ago. Today's data processing organizations are involved in every aspect of the company business, many of them in strategic and not just supporting roles. Long before outsourcing is considered, the client should review the placement of DP within the management structure and place it where it makes the most sense.

MIS organizations encompass many areas of responsibility, ranging from managing desktop systems to building strategic software systems to running existing software systems on large mainframes. Placing all of these functions under a single, generally unrelated area, like finance, for instance, makes no more sense than having each separate MIS area report directly to the president.

One approach gaining favor is the establishment of a chief information officer (CIO) who reports directly to the president and who owns all of the MIS organizations. This approach should be considered. However, since many organizations are very large and have many competing needs for MIS services, it might even be necessary to establish separate MIS facilities for each user area and have these groups cross-report to the CIO in addition to their user area.

Moving the MIS organizations into the user areas has risks that must be identified and addressed before the move. User areas traditionally question the amount of money needed by MIS and at times are loath to provide it. Agreements need to be made between the users controlling an MIS group and the corporate MIS organization regarding territorial boundaries. Corporate MIS must be allowed to preempt user decisions regarding technology whenever necessary and without amassing reams of supporting documentation (which is typically intentionally misunderstood by a foot-dragging user anyway). Also, having two reporting organizations, user and corporate MIS, introduces a problem with responsibility and authority.

Remove ALL Cross-Reporting Links

Employees who report to two bosses report to no boss. This controversial statement is not substantiated by any formal research and the authors of this book are split on its validity. The following point/counterpoint discussion provides both sides of this issue.

Point. Misquoting that old proverb "He who serves two masters serves none," brings the matter to a point. Many times employees receive conflicting instructions and priorities from a single manager. Indeed, priorities are almost always conflicting, and the great managers are those who consistently ferret out the best priority sequences. Two managers directing a single employee are bound to give the employee conflicting directions. When this happens the employee must choose between managers. Once the employee makes a choice, neither of the managers is managing from that point on. Their direction and priorities have just been upset.

Managers who have no control over their people cannot and will not accept responsibility for the work produced by the people. If a manager refuses to accept responsibility, the organization no longer has discipline, and without discipline the productivity of the organization declines.

Putting this bluntly, cross-management (or matrix management) naturally leads to fratricide among the organization. Fratricide leads to confusion and a lack of productivity. Confusion leads to a lack of visibility. And lack of visibility allows people to move up through the ranks using political skills (otherwise known as nepotism and "cult of the personality") rather than business and technical skills.

Counterpoint. The true issue is poor project planning, which results in over-allocation of personnel. Few managers develop project schedules, much less project plans that define scope, milestones, resource requirements, and priorities. It is imperative to establish basic project management methodologies to ensure that priorities are managed that mitigate personnel receiving conflicting priorities.

Managers have more than one boss if they provide services to more than one user. Each user is a boss with her own priorities. Managing priorities of multiple users is no different than managing the same pool of personnel for multiple work efforts.

There is a fundamental dichotomy between controlling a project and managing a project. The need to control a project is a reaction to unclear scope and requirements. Micromanaging will not improve personnel output.

If the focus is on managing the work, by default all attributes of a project will also be managed. The primary responsibilities of the manager are to balance work loads and meet or exceed user expectations. Project management is the only effective methodology for achieving these responsibilities.

Improve the Lines of Communication

The biggest impediment to performance outside of contradictory management directives is bad communication between MIS and the users and MIS and itself. Studies have shown that most cost and schedule overruns can be traced back to inadequate understanding of problem requirements. This is a direct consequence of bad communications.

There are several areas in which the lines of communication can be improved. Some involve technology, some involve documentation, some involve organizational structure, and some involve work habits and schedules. Each is discussed below.

Technology

With today's LAN technology and groupware products like Lotus Notes (and Domino), it is possible to provide up-to-date information on everything happening in MIS and make it available to everyone in both MIS and the user areas. Questions about project status, defect fixes, and availability should be on-line and real-time. Once everyone can see this information it will be possible to intelligently discuss and set priorities.

Technology also provides an impediment to productivity. Workstations are typically loaded up with word processors, project schedulers, database management packages, and spreadsheets. While each of these products has value to some people, rarely do they have value to all of the people. The use of these products by people who don't need them and are not trained in using them consistently leads to excessive usage time and effort. The classic example of this is the hours that people spend getting "just the right" fonts for the memo they are typing. Removing extraneous software tools from employee workstations will pay off in increased productivity. A new tool that is spreading quickly is employee access to the Internet. While it appears to be a must-have technology, there is no doubt that the Web browser, along with its Web surfing facility, is the biggest time waster corporate business has ever seen.

The point is simple. Don't make employees do what they don't do, and don't provide tools that are known to distract employees.

Documentation

Document everything using on-line tools that allow hypertext access to information. Keep employee profiles, project status, requirements, design documents, issues and solutions, and organization charts, all on-line. As the viewing tools associated with hypertext mature, users and MIS personnel alike will be able to issue queries against this information, and these queries will allow people to improve their performance.

An example of queries that would have value include the case where a manager wishes to know who is responsible for a given area. Usually this is the project leader, supervisor, or manager. But it could also be a senior analyst or even a programmer. A better example is the same query, only issued by an analyst in another area of MIS.

There are existing facilities, such as IBM's PROFS product, Lotus Notes, and Novell's GroupWise product, that provide some of this functionality. But the existing implementations using these products typically provide a fixed format for this information instead of a fully extendable, hypertext environment. (That said, Lotus Notes does provide a programming ability that can provide both the search and flexibility being proposed here.)

With many companies constructing internal web systems, or intranets, the use of hypertext technology is going to permeate the company. MIS should take advantage of this technology for its own gain.

Organizational Structure

Focus on single points of contact with well-defined responsibilities. Ignore trendy pseudo-technologies like employee empowerment, wall-less offices, and flat management structures. Each organization needs to concentrate on three attributes: knowledge retention, communication, and output. Organizations that maximize these three areas will not need to search for fads.

Each organization has a normal rate of employee turnover specific to the organization that influences its knowledge base. Occasionally this rate will temporarily increase or decrease. Once in a great while the normal rate will change up or down. When employees leave, the organization loses knowledge and experiences confusion. By concentrating on well-defined responsibilities, an organization can minimize the effect of losing employees.

Confusion and reduced output are consequences of poor communications. Communication usually involves the transfer of information, but outside the MIS environment it can also be considered the movement of materials. A look at the global depression that struck in the 1930s puts this in perspective. The amount of money available to the world did not change from 1920 to 1930, but the organizations distributing it failed, so the money could not move from entity to entity. And just as in the physical sciences where it is energy transfer (movement) that performs work, so it is that money transfer defines prosperity. In MIS information is money. Lines of communication define the prosperity of the organization.

> ## Confusion and Reduced Output Are the Consequences of Poor Communications.

Balancing this simplistic discussion is the effect of information overload. Many E-mail users find the amount of E-mail that they receive dominates their time. Simply filtering out which communications need reading from those that do not takes a substantial amount of time away from work. It is imperative that MIS minimize the amount of unnecessary information presented to the staff. Unnecessary information also confuses issues and can distort priorities. It is not uncommon to find people spending disproportionately large amounts of time on issues that have very small value. Organizations that can equate a value to each decision that must be made can reduce their costs tremendously.

(A new Internet technology just now entering service is called "push" technology. This technology will automatically send information to Web users. The natural consequence of this technology will be an increase in the instances of information overload. The use of push technology can best be used within the organization once formalized rules of usage are developed. MIS should not allow "pushed" information from outside the company to come unfiltered into the organization.)

Output from an organization is related to three factors: available expertise, general complexity of the environment, and energy of the staff. Young organizations, which usually consist of many young employees, often experience high levels of output. This is a natural consequence of running people at high energy levels (long hours, high excitement). The downside of these environments is that people can only perform at high levels for short periods of time before they burn out, and then they underperform. Organizations cannot count on high levels of energy and excitement to become the norm; they must prepare for a lower level of effort over a longer period of time. This is not a derogatory comment. In the world of physics, particularly energy generation, it is a known fact that a constant source of energy, such as constant winds that are not high velocity, provides more total energy than sporadic high bursts, such as gusting winds. Organizations must optimize their structure for constant throughput, with occasional bursts, rather than the opposite.

Constant Work Levels Give More Output Than Bursts of Work Separated by Lulls in Effort.

Work Habits and Schedules

The following suggestions sound extremely draconian. They are given because their benefits are grounded in fact. Each of these is based on maximizing the availability of personnel to others within the organization. Whether they are possible or not is another issue that needs to be addressed on an individual basis from company to company and department to department.

Remove flex hours and place everyone on the same schedule. Restrict lunch and break times to formal times. Reduce the amount and length of meetings.

Not all of these are possible. In the Los Angeles basin the local pollution control agencies mandate that companies must offer flex time to their employees. But the implementation of this is left to the employer. Organizations must minimize the amount of time that all of their staff are not available. Flex starting and stopping times reduce the amount of time during the day that information is guaranteed to be available to any employee asking for it. Flex days, implemented in 9 by 80 or 4 by 40 work schedules, where employees are not even present during one of the five week days, are particularly damaging. Some shops have so many employees missing on Mondays and Fridays and between 8 to 10 and 3 to 5 (and 11 to 1) that the organization is effectively available to perform work only three days a week from 10 to 11 in the morning and 1 to 3 in the afternoon, which is literally only 9 hours per week. (Before the reader convulses with laughter on this point, or adopts an air of sanctimonious disbelief, one author [Chapman] states that he has personal experience in such an organization and knows it to actually occur.)

If flex hours/days are mandated to MIS, the entire organization, with the exception of a user interface group, should honor the same exact schedule.

Meetings are a constant source of wasted time. It is not unusual for the management and senior personnel of an MIS department to spend so much time in meetings that they have no time to manage their staff. This is not a cliché. Meetings should be restricted to two uses. The first use is the dissemination of needed information and the second is the delegation of responsibilities and work schedules. Too many meetings are held because participants feel they need to meet as a normal part of their job. They lose sight of the fact that their first job is to be productive and that meetings were developed to assist them in that goal. Instead, many people view meetings as the output and work as something they do to prepare for a meeting. This mindset must be challenged and changed.

Appendix E

Trendy Development Tools and Their Legacy

Operations has seen an accelerating technology curve through the years. Equipment has become more reliable, has more capacity, and executes faster. In the software development area such has not been the case. COBOL, access methods, on-line transaction monitors, and database technology have provided a solid and smooth expansion of technical sophistication. But along the way MIS has always been looking for a silver bullet to speed its development efforts along. Many pretenders have come along and been quickly grasped by an unwitting MIS organization. Unfortunately, almost without exception these tools have turned into more of a hindrance than a benefit as time passed.

When an outsourcer takes over development or when functions are insourced, no stock should be put in the capacity of these nonstandard tools to reduce costs and increase functionality.

Development Tools Through Time

COBOL, FORTRAN, and machine languages have been available since the late 1950s. RPG and BASIC became available in the 1960s. Also during the 1960s, over 2,000 other languages were invented. Of those 2,000 languages, only PL/I is still with us in any measurable amount of use. Non-language tools have also come and gone over the last thirty years.

The following is a survey of the major non-language tools and also languages that have come and gone but have made an impact on the mainframe world. Notice during this discussion that a pattern is emerging through the years. That pattern is that these tools have a typical life span of about four years, after which it is almost impossible to find programmers capable of supporting systems written with them.

❖ *Mark IV from Informatics, 1970 to 1975.* Mark IV was supposed to remove the need for programmers in data processing. Mark IV was forms-based and supposedly easy to understand and use. Most Mark IV programs were small and easy to write. However, when Mark IV was used to develop detailed business systems, these programs became excessively large and required extremely talented individuals for support. By 1980 almost no Mark IV programmers were available on the market, and companies that had developed systems in Mark IV could no longer get the technical support necessary to continue its use in new systems.

❖ *Dyl260 – Dyl280 from Dylakor, 1975 to 1985.* Advertised as a tool to assist MIS in the creation of quick reports and useful utilities, these programs did just that. The products, which were forms-based at first and free-form later, allowed non-programmer users to build small systems with ease. Dylakor never marketed the Dyl2xx series of products as the solution to all development problems and as such enjoyed a profitable relationship with MIS. This is one of the few truly successful fourth generation tools in the market.

❖ *Focus from Information Builders, Inc., 1975 to present.* Focus has spread across many platforms during its life. Its major presence was back in the late 1970s to the early 1980s. Originally billed as a replacement for COBOL and other languages, its presence remains only in the user area where highly skilled non-programming programmers continue to use Focus. MIS departments are not capable of finding enough Focus programmers to enable its use in the development of new systems.

❖ *SAS from the SAS Institute, 1970s to present.* Billed as an early replacement for COBOL, it quickly found a niche in the creation and presentation of numerical data reports. SAS still maintains a presence by concentrating on its niche, but MIS found in the mid- to late 1980s that systems developed using SAS were becoming difficult to maintain as skilled programmers became harder and harder to find.

❖ *Easytrieve from Pansophic, 1985 to early 1990s.* Easytrieve was marketed as a replacement for COBOL. Easytrieve was supposed to remove the need for programmers and make systems development so easy that anyone could do it. Some companies migrated their Focus and SAS programs to Easytrieve. Today it is very hard to find Easytrieve programmers.

Moving down to the workstation brings in a new group of products. The workstation was pioneered by Digital Equipment Corp. back in the 1960s, but the technology really exploded into everyday usage with the introduction of the Intel 8088 (not the 8086) processor.

❖ *The BASIC language as implemented by IBM and Microsoft, 1981 to 1985.* Many systems were developed in BASIC by small companies, but not by most MIS departments. BASIC lacked a full feature set and thus could not provide all the tools necessary to support a full-service MIS department.

❖ *TurboPASCAL from Borland, 1985 to present.* One of the first of the popular languages on the workstation, many systems were developed in it. Most MIS shops avoided it; its main users seemed to be in academia and hobbyists.

❖ *dBASE I, II, III, and IV from Ashton Tate, 1985 to 1990.* dBASE was going to negate the need to use a formal programming language on the workstation platforms. Several copycat products were developed to exploit the market, FoxPro and R:BASE among others. While FoxPro and R:BASE are still being marketed today, it looks like FoxPro is losing support, and it is difficult to get experienced programmers for any of these products today.

❖ *Easel from Easel, 1989 to 1994.* Easel is still available but no longer is being enhanced. Easel's claim to fame was as one of the first GUI based 4GLs. Easel was to remove the need for programmers.

❖ *Applications Manager from Intelligent Environments, 1991 to present.* Applications Manager was going to replace the need for traditional programmers. While the product is still available and supported, it is very difficult to get experienced personnel.

❖ *Power Builder from Power Builder, 1993 to present.* Power Builder is marketed as a replacement for traditional development tools like COBOL. Power Builder's Achilles heel was its inability to seamlessly connect to relational databases. By merging with Sybase, Power Builder hoped to increase its marketability and prolong its life. Power Builder is still an actively supported product.

❖ *C from Lifeboat and then Microsoft, 1985 to present.* The first of the formal "super" languages. Marketed as the most powerful language ever developed, many commercial products were created in C. Some MIS departments used C for product development. However, it is instructive to note that at its peak of popularity C was denounced by its major originators, who have moved on to C++. C applications are now basically legacy applications, and the language's future is uncertain. The major marketer of C compilers, Microsoft, has publicly stated as far back as 1989 that they are developing BASIC as the language of the future.

❖ *Visual Basic, all its versions, from Microsoft, 1993 to present.* Microsoft markets Visual Basic as the language to replace all languages. VB 4 provides a lot of GUI support, including visual objects called controls, which are interchangeable and portable. VB 5 concentrates on improving the performance of the product.

❖ *JAVA from Sun, 1994 to present.* Java is hyped as being the language of the future. Java is platform independent and available from multiple vendors. One of Java's major claims to fame is that it uses a virtual machine implementation that frees it from the Microsoft operating environment. Very few Java programmers are available in today's marketplace. JAVA is a derivative of C++. If JAVA becomes popular it will mark the end of life for

C++. It already looks like C++ will be abandoned in favor of JAVA.

The most interesting observation to make from this short history lesson is that most of the tools mentioned above have had a very brief run of popularity. There are other tools which were not covered that also were thought to replace COBOL, but COBOL is still here and still being used by millions of programmers.

Before a company decides to adopt one of today's "super" languages such as C++ or Java, it should consider the impact four to five years in the future. Faced with the prospect of converting a system to another language five years after its creation or paying top dollar for programmers with antique and arcane skills, a visionary company would typically decide not to accept that circumstance. Thus, one should seriously question any proposal to adopt one of these nonstandard languages by either an outsourcer or a manager charged with insourcing.

The Durability of COBOL in the Business Environment

The biggest and most damning argument used against COBOL over the years has been its verbosity. People denigrate COBOL because it appears verbose. COBOL programs have a lot of "white space" in them, and the operands are spelled out in words instead of abbreviated with symbols. But a funny thing happened as technology changed and languages evolved. COBOL is no longer any more verbose than most other languages (with the possible exception of PL/I).

Back when "men were men and computers were computers" the major languages were COBOL and FORTRAN. FORTRAN allowed variable names to be only five characters long. COBOL allowed variable names to be up to thirty characters long. Following the old adage that what can be done will be done, COBOL programmers promptly made use of thirty-character variable names. Added to this verbosity was the use of words instead of symbols. An assignment statement in FOR-TRAN might read:

$$X = Y$$

While an assignment function in COBOL might read:

MOVE X TO Y.

Adding insult to injury in the verbosity category, the COBOL program would probably read something like this:

MOVE CURRENT BALANCE TO PREVIOUS BALANCE.

This example shows that COBOL is a verbose language. But is COBOL really verbose when compared with the other languages? What if the variable is not a numeric variable but instead contains character data or is an array? In this case FORTRAN and C start to show their own version of verbosity. In the late 1970s FORTRAN was enhanced to support long variable names, and this change put FORTRAN on exactly the same basis as C and COBOL in terms of variable name verbosity.

Assuming that the source variable contains 10 characters of text data the assignment statements for C and FORTRAN become the following:

FORTRAN

DO 10 I = 1,10
10   CurrentBalance(I) = PreviousBalance(I)

C

MEMCPY(PREVIOUS_BALANCE, CURRENT_BALANCE, 10);

While the COBOL assignment continues to read:

MOVE CURRENT BALANCE TO PREVIOUS BALANCE.

If the source variable was an array and the operation was an assignment the different languages would become:

FORTRAN

DO 10 I = 1,10
10   Current-Balance(I) = Previous-Balance(I)

C

FOR (I = 0; I <=9; I++)
{
Previous_Balance(I) = Current_Balance(I);
}

While the COBOL assignment continues to read:

MOVE CURRENT BALANCE TO PREVIOUS BALANCE.

Note that for character data, the C assignment is now more verbose than the COBOL statement, and so is the FORTRAN assignment. Plus, both C and FORTRAN continue to span multiple lines of code (which contain an iterated loop). For the array variables both the C and FORTRAN assignments become multistatement constructs. From this example, it is easy to see that once nonnumeric elementary variables are introduced, COBOL becomes much less verbose than either FORTRAN or C.

More important than the character and statement count judgment is the fact that the actual assignment statement type had to change in FORTRAN and C to accommodate the change in data type. The implication of this statement is simple. COBOL is simpler to use and thus is a simpler language than either FORTRAN or C. This means that COBOL is simpler to code (it requires fewer keystrokes than FORTRAN or C) and simpler to understand (it uses fewer statement types than FORTRAN or C).

The argument that COBOL is more verbose than FORTRAN and C is thus proved to be *FALSE.*

Lack of COBOL Programmers

The statement that colleges are not graduating COBOL programmers is true. It is also true that the institutions of higher learning have never graduated a significant number of COBOL programmers. Most of today's COBOL programmers were either trained on the job in programming or migrated from another language to COBOL. This is why COBOL has survived. COBOL is easy to learn and easy to use.

COBOL has about 100 reserved words that represent the command space available to the programmer. C and FORTRAN have much fewer reserved words, but they have more types of commands. C and FORTRAN also require that the programmer be constantly aware of the data type, while the COBOL compiler frees the COBOL programmer from this requirement. In short, COBOL is easy to learn because there is less to learn and easier to program in because the COBOL compiler does more work for the programmer than either C or FORTRAN.

How does COBOL compare to C++? The difference between COBOL and C++ is the same as between COBOL and C. COBOL supports metaclasses, classes, methods, and objects, just as C++ does. COBOL required an additional thirteen constructs to become object oriented. C required several hundred additional constructs in order to become C++. The disparity in the amount of changes to the base language highlights the difficulty of using C++ and the ease of using COBOL. COBOL is an easily extendable language, while C is not.

This same scenario of language evolution is repeated over and over again with the 4GL languages. Almost without exception, these 4GLs are extended by adding new constructs rather than extending the existing constructs. Users of these 4GLs are quickly overwhelmed by the additional exceptions to the language base, so maintenance becomes prohibitively difficult.

Once these facts are known, the prognosis is clear. COBOL is here to stay, and the other languages are transitory. 4GLs have a short life of popularity, sitting around four years. C is falling out of favor and is being replaced by C++. The complexity of C++ works against its future and means that eventually it will be replaced by another *evolutionary* improvement. Visual Basic is already on its way out as Microsoft touts yet another new language (Visual JAVA) as the language of the future. JAVA, the newest language, will be jettisoned once the Microsoft threat to the platform industry is either thwarted or consolidated. COBOL is the only language that will stay the course.

Appendix F
Workstation Tools for the Job

Workstation tools is an inflammatory area for discussion. Two disparate views prevail in today's industry. One view is that each workstation should have every tool imaginable on it so that the developer is a self-contained unit. The other view is that workstation software should be limited to only those items that are directly germane to the tasks at hand. Reconciling these views may not be possible. On the one hand, having the right tool for the job makes the job easier. On the other hand, having many tools means learning and mastering (note that there is a difference between the two attributes) each tool, and this can require a significant investment in time and money.

Trade-offs are a part of any decision. No company has an unlimited amount of time and money. No organization has an unlimited amount of expertise. The following review touches on each of the important categories of workstation tools, discusses pros and cons and assesses the costs associated with the tool.

The point that becomes most clear about tools on the workstation is that only those tools that are actually needed for the tasks at hand should be present on a workstation. Personnel should also be performing only those tasks that they are trained to perform. For instance, programmers are not known for their ability to compose prose. Programmers need tools in order to document their work and communicate their technical ideas. But programmers mainly need a good program source editor. Turning a programmer into a graphics artist, author, or accountant is a money-losing proposition. But by including tools that are geared to these activities, management has extended the programmers' job description and thrust them into an area where they have no expertise. This immediately leads to higher costs for those "nonprimary" functions.

The subtle implication of the proliferation of inappropriate tools is replacement of specialized staff with laymen. Secretaries and typing pools are replaced by managers and executives. Graphics artists are replaced by managers and programmers. Accountants are replaced by front-line managers and senior analysts. In each case the costs associated with the replacement are substantially higher than one would expect.

Word Processors

Word processors are the ubiquitous tools that moved workstations onto the desks of the non-programming staff. In the hands of a skilled individual, a word processor is a formidable tool. Good, clean communication skills are amplified by the word processor. Skilled use of words, fonts, and graphics can present concepts, facts, and commands in clear and understandable terms. While many people think that spreadsheets legitimized the personal computer market, they are ignoring the fact that typing and communication are the main work activity of the typical office worker. Spreadsheets are great for doing *spreadsheets,* but few of the repetitive office tasks deal with spreadsheets.

One problem with word processors is that many people use them excessively. Another problem is that they do not make confusing communications any less confusing. Now would be a good time to remember that not everyone can clearly express the concepts and ideas that they are attempting to communicate. Clear communication often relies on the efforts of several people. One person writes, another clarifies the ideas, a third may restructure the grammar. Since writing clear communications has typically been a multiperson endeavor, it is appropriate to ask the following question: What is wrong with everyone using a word processor?

The answer is simple. Clear communication requires clear thinking, not clear text. Reviewing the documents generated by many people provides a solid indication of the difficulty of communicating clearly. Many executives have started composing and creating their own memos. These memos frequently contain ambiguities and typographic errors. Also, it is apparent from the errors in the documents that the author cannot type. This means that executives are spending more time than necessary to create the document and are not effectively getting their messages across.

What is wrong with everyone using a word processor? Using a word processor costs too much in wasted time and miscommunication.

Spreadsheets

Spreadsheets propelled Apple Computer to fame and fortune in the early 1980s. VisiCalc, the first major spreadsheet program, demonstrated the use of a cell-based, repetitive programming language. Lotus, with its 1-2-3 product, integrated spreadsheet, graphics, and word processing technology into one package for use with IBM PC compatible systems. "It's as easy as 1-2-3" became a truism once Lotus 1-2-3 hit the streets. From that point on everyone needed to introduce a spreadsheet. In today's market the big spreadsheets are Microsoft Excel, Lotus 1-2-3, and Corel.

Who needs a spreadsheet on their workstation? Almost no one, it turns out. Spreadsheets are typically used to generate and process tabular data. By using graphics capabilities, these tables are turned into graphs. The graphs can be annotated with the word processing features. But word processors also contain table processing capabilities and graphics capabilities. So, with some notable exceptions, most of the attributes of a spreadsheet can be supplied by a word processor. The spreadsheet part of spreadsheets is usually used to automate simple application calculations.

If a workstation contains a word processor, there is almost no need for a spreadsheet. If a workstation contains a spreadsheet, there is almost no need for a word processor. While accountants and auditors can use spreadsheets to their best advantage, most people cannot be counted on to learn enough about the spreadsheet program to be anything other than a burden on their coworkers.

Presentation Software

The ability to generate a presentation on demand fueled the sales of these products during the last five years. There was a time when a mainstream presentation graphics package would run $400. This was also true of the word processors and spreadsheets. People were not buying presentation graphics software because they had no need for it. Very few people are marketing reps who need to make presentation after presentation. As a way to expand market share and to prevent competitors from buying a competing product, presentation graphics packages began to appear in application suites. Soon everyone had a presentation graphics package on their workstation.

Given that most people don't give presentations, it is legitimate to ask what presentation graphics packages are good for. They could be used to organize thoughts, but a paper and pencil would probably be more effective. The president of Sun Microsystems, when asked how the company managed an 18 percent gain in profit in 1996, said, "We removed all the (vendor name here...) presentation graphics packages and our productivity went through the roof."

Terminal Emulators

Contrary to the impression one gets from reading the trade press, most development personnel are associated with work on mainframes. Rather than use real terminals, these developers now access the host through terminal emulation software. The benefit of this approach is that the terminal emulators typically support multiple host sessions. This allows the developer to maintain an edit/compile session and a test session simultaneously. This ability to manage multiple simultaneous sessions improves programmer productivity.

Terminal emulators were the best thing to happen to mainframe programmers since the move from punch cards to CRTs. Terminal emulators are natural candidates for replacement by the newly announced Network Computers (NC). Considering that there are some 20 million terminal and terminal emulator sessions out in the world, the NC is poised for a successful future. Since NCs have no user-accessible moving parts, they are no more prone to breakage than real terminals, but they are much more powerful. More important than the physical reliability of the devices is the fact that users cannot load software onto the NC. They must use software residing in or installed from the server. Add to this that workstations running terminal emulators are the most expensive platforms available for mainframe access. Considering that a real terminal could be leased for under $10 per month and that the annual maintenance cost of a workstation runs at several thousand dollars, it is easy to find a financial benefit to NCs. The sooner MIS replaces workstations with NCs, the better for all concerned.

Web Browsers

Web browsers that are connected to the Internet have no place in an MIS environment unless they are tightly controlled. Internet access is not a boon to developers; it is an incredible time waster. Web browsers used as front ends to on-line systems are another matter. Using a Web browser as the user interface vehicle for an on-line system raises the productivity of both the development team and the user area.

Virtually every major on-line system is offering "on the fly" conversion from the native terminal input/output to HTML format. This conversion enables the terminal communication system to make use of every Internet system as a potential terminal interface. Providing both a graphical user interface and a consistent command structure using HTML, the Web browser is quickly becoming the universal terminal interface.

The downside of the Web browser is the current attempt by the major software vendors to introduce proprietary extensions that lock users into one hardware/software platform or another. The uncertainty brought on by these tactics is causing some companies to hold off choosing a Web browser standard. If a company generates its own HTML-based Web pages, it can make itself immune to this battle by intentionally supporting only those HTML constructs that are accepted as standard features by all competing parties. Unfortunately, a complete sabotage of the HTML standards could be a side effect of the browser wars.

Several operating system vendors are making noises about replacing their existing graphical user interfaces with Web browsers. Some companies are talking about using JAVA, a portable language/virtual machine combination that is typically integrated into a Web browser, as a way to free the user community from the existing proprietary operating systems. The argument in favor of this is that if your interface is a Web browser and is JAVA-based you do not have to see the native operating system interfaces, and so any underlying operating system is acceptable.

In a related development discussed under the Multimedia category on page 185, voice recognition is now available as a standard feature of OS/2 based Web browsers.

Development Languages

The major languages available for workstation platforms today are COBOL, C, C++, Visual Basic, and FORTRAN. Also found, but in much smaller numbers, are Smalltalk, BAL (or Assembler), and PL/I. Several languages that looked like they were going to make a big impact in development environments were

Pascal and Forth, but these languages are now dead. One special case language, Ada, which is used for embedded processing, could have moved out of the defense industry and into the commercial area, but did not. The interesting question is, what happens in a multiple language environment? Is there an impact on the ability of an organization to deliver software systems when multiple languages are in use? And how does this affect the workstation environment?

The truth about development is this. As the environment becomes more complicated, the ability of the average MIS personnel to perform work decreases. This decrease takes shape in two forms. First, as more tools are added to the workstation, more time is spent administering to the tools. Contrary to what seems to be the case at first glance, a lot of time is spent keeping these tools functional on each desktop. It is not unusual for a workstation to be incapacitated for one or more days when a tool upgrade is applied. Multiply this by the number of workstations and the time of the technicians to administer the upgrades and the total becomes important.

Even more important, each additional tool requires more expertise from the MIS staff. It may be sad, but it is certainly true that many people already do not know enough about their development toolset. For example, in the IBM MVS mainframe environment, it is not unusual for a large percentage of the development staff to have trouble with JCL, not know how CICS works, not understand the performance ramifications of a DB2 design, not be able to define VSAM files, and not even know how to transfer files from the mainframe to the workstation. On the workstation, the level of ignorance is even greater.

Once a workstation starts to contain all of the same types of facilities as the mainframe, this ignorance is simply transferred to the workstation environment. Just because users now have their own copy of CICS does not mean that they know how to use it. Another example is file systems. Many people don't understand mainframe files; when they move to workstations they don't understand workstation files; and when they move to DB2, for example, they don't understand DB2, workstation files, or mainframe files. The ignorance simply compounds.

The lesson is simple: don't put development tools on a workstation unless they are needed for the tasks at hand. When the tasks are finished it is probably wise to remove the tool.

One final point is that often development tools interfere with one another. After installing a new development tool it is not unusual to find that an existing development tool has ceased to function correctly. This occurs all the time. Each occurrence of this type of problem increases the cost of each development tool. If an organization reduces the number of tools on the workstation, it also reduces the administrative burden, the downtime, the confusion, and the workstation cost.

Database Systems

The new office suites being offered for workstations are now offered with consumer-oriented database systems. These database systems have a lot of flash in the user interface, but are about ten years behind in the database technology area. The consequences of this are amazing. Mainframe database technology has concentrated on two areas over its life span. First, much effort has been put into making the database system execute quickly and efficiently. Second, even more effort has been put into ensuring the integrity of the data maintained in the database.

Workstation databases that have evolved from the consumer side of the industry have concentrated on ease of use and the graphical user interface. In many cases the entire effort to provide data integrity boils down to suggesting that the consumer reload the database from the backup. Reloading a database from backups is not normally an acceptable action in a business system. Thus, most businesses putting database software on their workstations will want to use those database products that have migrated down from the mainframe, rather than up from the workstation. The point here is that reliability is much more important than a slick user interface when business issues are considered. Reliability cannot be bolted onto a product after development; it has to be fully integrated into it.

Database software is developing into major resource users. It is not unusual for a workstation database product to require 32 MB of RAM or more to run effectively. These systems are also placing much greater burdens on the CPU and I/O subsystems. While CPUs are getting faster every day to the extent that one can now get 4-way 200 MIPS processors in a workstation, there has been no such advance in the I/O bandwidth of the workstation. Thus, even though the processing is quick, the retrieval of data from large databases is throttled by the I/O bandwidth of the workstation.

The most important ramification of workstation databases is not the added burden they place on the CPU or the I/O bandwidth. It is the feeling by the developers that since they can define tables and databases on their workstations they must, therefore, be database designers. Many mainframe projects have run into major problems caused by programmers considering themselves to be designers. This problem is compounded by the workstation environment. Not only can a programmer develop a bad database architecture; the power of the workstation usually hides the database design defects. Performance problems are not seen on the test workstations, but appear when the system enters real-life testing or is placed in production. Database contention and massive search sequences show up only when production-sized volumes are run though the systems. It is not unusual for the programmers to find they have absolutely no clue as to why the production system executes processing requests so slowly that the system is considered worthless by the user community.

CASE Tools

CASE, or Computer Aided Software Engineering, tools were a hot technology area in the late 1980s to early 1990s. Since then, they have not received much publicity. The original tools fell into two categories. The first were analytically centric, and the second were code generation centric. Many of the companies developing and marketing CASE tools have withdrawn from the marketplace.

CASE tools represent an attempt to formalize the development process. They have been superseded by the new super languages, C++ and JAVA. This does not mean that C++ and JAVA offer more value than CASE, just that they have captured the mind share and purchasing dollars of most organizations.

CASE has the ability to reduce development time and the related costs. But CASE has not been an easy technology to acquire and implement, and therein lies the problem. A developer can buy a C++ compiler for $500 or get a JAVA compiler for free, and in either case be generating supposedly reusable code within a couple of hours. A user of CASE tools, especially the analytical ones, must spend $50,000 and up, then spend years becoming proficient. The cost and learning curves are enough to make CASE move out of the limelight.

The bottom line is that CASE tools have not yet proved that they have value to an organization when all factors are considered. These factors—cost, time to market, reusability, learning curve, and reliability—have different levels of importance in different organizations. In fact, if history demonstrates anything, it is that people will jump for the short-term advantage at the expense of the long-term good. So CASE probably will only be successfully adopted by MIS if the price and learning effort drop substantially.

Groupware

Groupware consists of several types of products whose only similarity lies in the adoption of the name. For instance, Lotus has two products that epitomize groupware: Notes and Domino. Intranets and Internets are also a form of groupware. Lotus has a suite of products called SmartSuite which includes a groupware-oriented word processor called WordPro. Other office suites are coming out with similar products.

What is groupware? It is hard to say specifically, but generally groupware products provide tools that allow groups of people to work on development, correspondence, or documentation in tandem instead of individually. With the exception of the Notes and Domino products, there seems to be no real substance to the term. Instead, the marketing engines of several companies seem to be attempting to siphon business dollars off the periphery of the Lotus products.

Multimedia

Multimedia, which is the combination of sound, animation, video, and graphics, is a potent combination. Using multimedia in a product can increase the efficiency in which information is conveyed to individuals and groups. As such, it is an exciting technology for user systems. But there is currently very little justification for multimedia on MIS systems. Its biggest impact so far seems to be the ability to drive coworkers to distraction with the strange sounds that emanate from computers.

Sound and video are currently not being used effectively in the MIS and operations environments. Thus, any sound and video facilities on a workstation are apt to be used almost entirely for entertainment value. That being said, an entirely new development may change the value of multimedia forever. The latest release of OS/2 (Warp 4) comes with speaker-independent voice recognition with a 20,000-word vocabulary built in. This facility is currently being used extensively by handicapped MIS personnel. It is only a matter of a short time before this technology begins to be pervasive in all user interfaces. After all, GUIs are currently visual and tactile, so their extension into the vocal arena would be a natural extension.

Voice recognition is moving into the workstation environment at a fast pace. Already two of the major Web browsers are voice enabled, and the voice technology is available on two operating system platforms (OS/2 and Windows 95). The extension of this technology to other platforms is already underway. Windows NT will soon have this IBM technology, while the two other major voice vendors, Dragon Systems and Kurzweil Artificial Intelligence, already have Windows NT and Windows 95, but not OS/2, products.

Appendix G

Pricing Trends in Hardware and How to Take Advantage of Them

Predicting the course of hardware evolution is difficult at best and hazardous at worst. One thing is perfectly clear. Hindsight is 20-20 and in business, where saving money is often the equivalent of earning money, looking to the past is a valid technique for planning the future. By reviewing the hardware pricing trends of the past, it should be possible to provide generally accurate short-term predictions for the future. This appendix looks at hardware scaling and pricing through the last thirty years. While it is possible that a new technology may pop up and invalidate the trends extracted from viewing the past, it is also clear that any change will be for the better rather than for the worse.

1960s—The Formative Years

The introduction of the System 360 series of processors by IBM in the early 1960s heralded two new trends in the computer industry: common hardware designs as seen by the programmer and software compatibility, both forward and backward. Prior to the advent of the System 360 line of computers from IBM, each processor was generally incompatible with its predecessors and its peers. With the System 360 line came a common set of operating systems, OS/MFT, OS/MVT, and DOS. These operating systems also were compatible; application programs written for the OS/Mxx operating systems were generally interchangeable, while DOS programs were compatible within the S/360 line. It is interesting to note that these three operating systems still exist. OS/MFT and OS/MVT have evolved into OS/390, while DOS has evolved into VSE/ESA.

The System 360 computer line consisted of the models 30, 40, 50, and 65. Several variations on these models were introduced, variations that stressed different parts of the System 360 architecture. For instance, a model 44 was introduced that provided substantially better arithmetic performance than the base model 40.

These processors ranged from 250 KIPS for the model 40 up to 1 MIPS for the model 65. Memory sizes ranged from 32 KB up to a high of 1 MB of core memory. On-line systems were starting to evolve using formed character terminal/printer units (paper-based output devices).

The OS operating system family made movement between processor models easy for commercial customers, especially along the hardware upgrade path. While there were a few exceptions, in the main, the peripheral hardware devices were compatible from processor model to model. As a result, commercial customers were in a position for the first time in history of being able to upgrade individual parts of their systems without obsoleting the other parts.

1970s—Virtual Memory and Large Address Spaces

The early 1970s saw the introduction of the System 370 (S/370) line of processors. These processors had three major advances over the S/360 line: virtual memory, semiconductor memory, and a high level of semiconductor integration. The ramifications of these features were simple. Virtual memory allowed software systems to be designed in a more robust environment because the developers were freed of memory constraints. Semiconductor memory allowed the manufacturing techniques used in semiconductors to be used in manufacturing memory. (Remember that prior to semiconductor memory, core memory was actually hand-threaded, donut-shaped ferrite cores.) Higher levels of semiconductor integration allowed for higher clock cycles, thus making faster processors possible.

The S/370 family consisted of three original models, the 145, 155, and 165, which were quickly replaced with the 148, 158, and 168. The difference was the hardware implementation of virtual memory (which was not implemented in the original three models). The 148 weighed in around .5 MIPS, the 158 was 1 MIPS, and the 168 was around 3 MIPS. These processor speeds, combined with the increased memory spaces allowed by both virtual memory and semiconductor memory technology, provided the basis for extending the processing arena that a computer system could address.

Also introduced with the S/370 158 and 168 models was the MP, or multiprocessor, configuration. The S/370 158MP processor combined two 1 MIPS 158 processors into a tightly coupled processor complex where main memory was shared between the two processors and a couple of machine instructions were introduced to facilitate the synchronization of processes on the two processors. The combined throughput of these MP configurations was about 1.78 times that of a single processor.

Along with the MP configuration came a more sophisticated version of the OS/Mxx operating systems called MVS. MVS could run up to 2048 processes, called address spaces, on a single processor. Each address space appeared to be a complete machine all by itself. MVS introduced a set of management tools designed to increase the throughput of the processing system. In other words, the operating system moved from simply assisting programs in accessing machine resources to managing those resources for maximum utilization.

At the same time that MVS made its debut, another IBM operating system was being developed, VM. VM used the S/370 processor complex in another way. Rather than providing a sophisticated set of facilities for the programs to call on, it provided a simple programming support system (based on the S/360 based OS/Mxx operating system rather than MVS) and concentrated on maximizing hardware throughput overall.

These two operating systems are still with us today, and both are attempting to get the most out of the hardware facilities.

As the S/370 line was making its appearance, another innocuous device was being manufactured, the Intel 4004 and 8008 microprocessors. By 1976 the Intel 8080 had made its appearance. This microprocessor could address 64 KB memory spaces and had an instruction set that was designed around the ability to fabricate logic gates in an integrated circuit environment. The consequence of this physical limitation of the manufacturing techniques led to a microprocessor instruction set that was the minimum necessary to create a full-function processor. Specifically, it constrained the number of registers and thus forced the Intel processor to implement an accumulator-based instruction set rather than a register-based instruction set.

With the popularity of the Intel 8080 microprocessor came a clone named the Zilog Z80, which had a somewhat more sophisticated instruction set that under some circumstances ran faster than the Intel 8080. Its biggest benefits were a faster clock speed and a better instruction set. The Intel 8080 and the Z80 microprocessors formed the basis for the first personal computers on the market, the IMSAI 8080 and the Tandy/Radio Shack TRS-80. The TRS-80 is notable in that it provided a complete Z80-based, 4 KB RAM system including display and keyboard for $600. Over 1 million of these systems were sold in the first year (1978; for those of us with perfect hindsight this was a solid indication of the PC revolution to come).

In 1976 IBM released another generation of the S/370 family, the 3033. This processor had a base speed of 3.5 MIPS and ranged up to 5 MIPS as additional model types were announced over the next four years. The 3033 line had a designed-in virtual memory facility and a more normalized ability to run in an MP configuration. The 3033 also introduced a further abstraction of the I/O systems, which were now controlled by Directors. Directors were basically 1 MIPS processors (about the size and power of a S/370 158) that sat between the CPU and the I/O channels. Adding Directors to the I/O design enhanced the ability of the processor complex to maximize the I/O throughput of the system.

1980s—The Revolution Starts

The 1980s were the birth of today's computing environment. While most people associate this time with the personal computer revolution, there was actually another revolution happening in the big system arena: multiprocessor technology. Many industry pundits were forecasting processing limits for processor technology. To address this theoretical brick wall, mainframe designers started concentrating on connecting CPUs and processor complexes together. So in the 1980s computer technology started extending both up and down, giving the phrase "power to the people" a whole new meaning.

Seymour Cray introduced his Cray-I computer systems, which used parallel floating point processors to achieve the astounding rate of 80 Million Floating Point Instructions per Second (MFLOPS) under ideal conditions. Even more startling was that the business community started to see uses for supercomputers and started placing orders for them. Prior to the Cray I, most supercomputer sales took place to government agencies. Even at $20 million a pop the Cray I was cost effective.

IBM introduced the S/370 3080 series of processors. These processors, based on a 6 MIPS CPU engine, also contained the 3084, a four processor model. Two items of significance came with these models. First, the MIPS rating for a single engine went as high as 10 MIPS. Second, the MP architecture was successfully extended to a four-processor environment. In less than fifteen years the effective power of a computer processor complex went from 1 MIPS (S/360 model 65) to 25 MIPS (S/370 model 3084). Even as the power was going up, the cost of the processor complexes was staying about the same (in 1970 dollars).

In 1981 IBM also introduced the IBM Personal Computer. This PC was based on the Intel 8088 microprocessor and had a MIPS rating of about .1. In 1983 IBM added a 10 MB hard disk to that PC and called it the IBM PC/XT. With this addition Intel 8088-based personal computers became a viable technology for small business users. In 1985 IBM introduced the IBM PC/AT personal computer based on the Intel 80286 microprocessor. The Intel 80286 microprocessor supported multiple address spaces and up to 16 MB of virtual memory. This personal computer ran three times faster than the Intel 8088-based computers and achieved about .3 MIPS of processing power. In 1987 Intel introduced the 80386 processor, which extended the virtual memory space of the 80286 into the terabyte range, and the MIPS rating reached 1 MIPS. In 1988 Intel introduced the 80486 microprocessor, which ran three times faster than the Intel 8086 microprocessor and increased the MIPS rating above 3.

Intel-based microprocessors were now rivaling the mainframe processors in base MIPS. With extremely fast microprocessors available, the PC revolution seemed poised to destroy the mainframe processor market.

1990s—The Mainframe Strikes Back

In the late 1980s and early 1990s it looked like the Intel microprocessor-based personal computers were going to remove the need for mainframes. IBM did not take this threat lightly. The System 390 computer line was introduced in the late 1980s, offering a base MIPS rate of 11 and scalable to 6 tightly coupled processors. Over the next five years IBM raised the MIPS rating of the individual processors up to 52 IBM's plug-compatible competitors raised the MIPS ratings up to 84. Mainframe processor complexes could now reach 300 to 500 MIPS.

Intel was not sitting still while these mainframe improvements were being made. Intel announced the Pentium processor, the next generation of the 80486 microprocessor line. The Pentium processor, in its various releases (including the Pentium

Pro) currently scales up to 200 MIPS. Then Intel started introducing multiprocessor implementations of the Pentium processor, allowing up to four Pentium processors in one processor complex, giving a theoretical processor power of 800 MIPS.

But the personal computer system suffers from an Achilles' heel: low I/O throughput. While a 1 MIPS S370/158 from 1975 could process some 1 GB (1 billion bytes) of data through its I/O system per second, an 800 MIPS Pentium processor complex still struggles to sustain 2 MB per second.

In 1994 IBM struck again at the Intel processor juggernaut. IBM released CMOS-based System 390 processors capable of running at 10 MIPS, which could be placed into a 64-processor complex. In 1996, only two years later, IBM doubled this MIPS rating to 20. At the end of 1996 IBM started shipping 40 MIPS CMOS processors. Putting these CMOS processors into complexes of 64 processors or more allowed IBM to counter the MIPS weakness while still maintaining the 1000-to-1 advantage in I/O bandwidth. Mainframe IBM systems can now scale past 2400 MIPS, with no upper bound in sight.

Recapping the History of Processing Power

IBM has released new processor technology every five years. Intel has released new microprocessor technology every three years. The cost of each new generation at its introduction remains the same (when considering constant dollars) or less. With each new generation, the cost of the previous generation drops by more than half. Software costs have also decreased. People costs have remained constant (again using constant dollars).

With one notable exception, almost every company in the computer industry strives for compatibility in its products from one generation to another. Generally customers can expect that programs and hardware acquired for their current hardware system can be used unchanged in the next hardware generation. This statement may not be valid for a two-generation change.

If you make the assumption that the highest capacity systems remain at the same inflation adjusted price while reviewing the following hardware capacity tables, you will get a good feeling for how technology has evolved in the past and will evolve in the future. Since 1980 IBM has maintained three families of System 370/390 processors. These families address the large corporate customer, the midsize corporate customer, and the small, or satellite, corporate customer. The large customer needed a raised floor environment and water cooling equipment. The midsize customer needed a raised floor. The small and satellite customer need only floor space. In today's environment, the water cooled requirement is disappearing, so the large- and medium-size customers will be using the same product line and will be differentiated only by the number of processors each uses.

Large Customer Mainframes

1975	S/370-158	1 MIPS
1977	S/370-3033	3.5 MIPS
1981	S/370-3081	1 MIPS
1983	S/370-3083	6 MIPS
1990	S/390-180	17 MIPS
1993	9221-900	250 MIPS

Midsize Customer Mainframes

1980	4341	1 MIPS
1985	4381	3.5 MIPS
1987	4381MP	7 MIPS

Small Customer Mainframes

1979	4331	< 1 MIPS
1981	4361	< 1 MIPS
1995	S500-P390	3.5 MIPS
1996	S520-P390	3.5 MIPS, more I/O capacity
1996	R6000-P390	3.5 MIPS, even more I/O capacity

Merged Large and Midsize Company Mainframes		
1994	S/390 CMOS	10 MIPS up to 4 processors
1995	S/390 CMOS	20 MIPS up to 16 processors
1996	S/390 CMOS	40 MIPS up to 64 processors

The lesson here is fairly straightforward. People costs are constant and processor power is getting cheaper. Companies can safely remain one generation back in computer power and still remain functional. Companies that drop back two generations are starting to incur a compatibility risk.

If a company can manage its processor requirements growth, substantial savings can be made by staying one generation back. In fact, an entire leasing industry has formed around this concept. Companies that have traditionally been users of first generation equipment should seriously consider previous generation hardware when they are insourcing.

If an outsourcing agreement has spanned five years, the hardware prices for the equipment in use at the beginning will probably range from 10 to 20 percent of the original price.

Appendix H
Related Reading

The reading list provides a broad base of information for those who wish to draw their own conclusions on the topics covered in this book. This list should only be considered a starting point.

Anderson, T. W. and Jeremy D. Finn. *The New Statistical Analysis of Data*. New York: Springer-Verlag, 1996.

Davis, Alan M. *201 Principles of Software Development*. New York: McGraw-Hill, Inc., 1995.

Farson, Richard. *Management of the Absurd*. New York: Simon & Schuster, 1996.

Fried, Louis. *Managing Information Technology in Turbulent Times*. New York: John Wiley & Sons, Inc., 1995.

Gunton, Tony. *A Dictionary of Information and Computer Science*. Oxford, England: Penguin Books Limited, 1990.

Humphrey, Watts S. *A Discipline for Software Engineering*. Reading, Mass.: Addison-Wesley Publishing Company, 1995.

Jenner, Michael G. *Software Quality Management and ISO 9000*. New York: John Wiley & Sons, Inc., 1995.

Johnson, Perry L. *ISO 9000: Meeting the New International Standards*. New York: McGraw-Hill, Inc., 1993.

Kern, Harris and Randy Johnson. *Rightsizing the New Enterprise*. Mountain View, Calif.: SunSoft Press, 1994.

King, Patricia. *Never Work for a Jerk*. New York: Dell Publishing, 1987.

Lacity, Mary C. and Rudy Hirscheim. *Information Systems Outsourcing, Myths, Metaphors and Realities*. Chichester, West Sussex, England: John Wiley & Sons, Ltd., 1993.

Lacity, Mary C. and Rudy Hirscheim. *Beyond the Information Systems Outsourcing Bandwagon, The Insourcing Response.* Chichester, West Sussex, England: John Wiley & Sons, Ltd., 1995.

Schlesinger, Phyllis F., Vijay Sathe, Leonard A. Schlesinger, and John P. Kotter. *Organization: Text, Cases, and Readings on the Management of Organizational Design and Change.* Homewood, Ill.: Richard D. Irwin, Inc., 1979, 1986, and 1992.

Schneider, William E. *The Reengineering Alternative.* Burr Ridge, Ill.: Richard D. Irwin, Inc., 1994.

Index

wasted time, 177
Web browsers, 179–180, 185
weighted grade profile, 156
weighted on-line availability,
    148–149
weighted report availability,
    147
weighted service level, 144
Windows 95, 186
Windows NT, 186

WordPro, 184–185
word processors, 176–177
work habits, 164–165
workstation tools, 175–186
wrong equipment mix, 9

yesterday's technology, 54

Z80, 190
Zilog, 190